FOOD FOR THE FED-UP

G. A. STUDDERT KENNEDY

M.C. , H.C.F.

British Library Cataloguing In Publication Data
A Record of this Publication is available
from the British Library

ISBN 978-1-84685-826-0

Published 2007 by
Diggory Press
an imprint of
Diggory Press Ltd
Three Rivers, Minions, Liskeard, Cornwall, PL14 5LE, UK
and of Diggory Press, Inc.,
Goodyear, Arizona, 85338, USA
WWW.DIGGORYPRESS.COM

TO
J. K. MOZLEY, B.D.
GRATITUDE FOR MANY YEARS
OF FIRM FRIENDSHIP,
AND MANY LESSONS LEARNED

Author's Foreword

THIS odd book rests upon an assumption. It is not odd because of that. Most books do. They have to, because all thought rests upon assumptions. If in this life you refuse to assume anything you had better blow out your brains or take some prussic acid. Committing suicide is like docking small dogs' tails - it is better to do it all at once than by inches. I have assumed that the hall-mark of the modern mind which separates it from the mind of yesterday is the idea of progress, the conception of man and man's world as being unfinished things which are in process of creation. What has happened in modern times is that the idea of progress has become so dominant and powerful and so widely spread that we must either think out and express our religion in terms of that idea, or go without one altogether. Dean Inge says that the idea of progress is not a modern one, but so ancient as to be almost played out. I hate differing from the Dean - he knows so much that ordinary people cannot differ from him without having an uneasy sensation that they are probably fools. But one has to put up with that - and anyhow I am used to it, I have had it all my life. And besides, it cannot really be helped; however much he may hate to differ from the Dean, the ordinary man cannot possibly agree with him without going melancholy mad, and on the whole it is better to live in a Fool's Paradise than to die in the county lunatic asylum.

And so, in spite of the Dean, I still make my assumption: the idea of progress although individuals among the ancients may have had it in their minds and expressed it is essentially a modern idea, and *the* essential modern idea. It has filtered through from the study to the street, and has taken hold, not merely of the intellectual, but of the ordinary man who works with his hands to keep his children. And in that form - the popular form - it is entirely modern. The point is: is it true? The Dean in his Romanes lecture seems to think that on the whole it is not. I am bound to confess that I find the Romanes lecture dreadfully confusing; I dare not say that it is confused. Half my time I am wondering whether the Dean is cursing the idea of mechanical and inevitable progress in the macrocosmos, or the ordinary common or garden idea of possible progress in the cosmos. I am a bit vague as to what the macrocosmos is, and quite clear that whatever it is I do not know anything about it. The Dean says that the idea of progress in the macrocosmos is untenable and incompatible with Christianity, and I am quite willing to take his word for it, but I am grateful to him for the statement that 'there may be an infinite number of finite purposes, some much greater and others much smaller than the span of an individual life, and within each of these some divine thought may be working itself out, bringing some life or series of lives, some nation or race or species, to that perfection which is natural to it - what the Greeks called its "nature." ... It may be that there is an imminent teleology which is shaping the life of the human race towards some completed development which has not yet been reached.'

That really gives me all I need. What the Dean calls an 'imminent teleology' I would be content to call God, or, in the language of St. John's Gospel, 'the Word of God by Whom all things were made.' Incidentally, I cannot help feeling that God is not merely a simpler, but a more accurate, term to use, because teleology implies a person to teleologise, unless we are to believe in a mechanical teleology which the Dean says (and I agree - Hurrah! I am not a fool any longer now) is anathema. The fact of the matter is that the popular idea of progress has nothing to do with the macrocosmos, or any such remote questions as those which concern its ultimate nature. It has only to do with the human race and the possibility of its progress towards perfection; and this the Dean allows is an essentially modern idea, for he admits that 'on the whole the ancients did tend to regard Time as the enemy. ... They would have thought the modern notion of human perfectibility at once absurd and impious.' The idea that has taken hold of us all is that there is a meaning and a purpose that runs through human history as a whole, and that the great call of God to human beings is to discover what that purpose is, and co-operate with Him in working it out. The great value of the Dean's lecture seems to me to lie in its vigorous protest against the idea that you can progress without knowing where you are going to; that you can co-operate in the working out of God's purpose without in any way understanding what the purpose is; that the new doctrine is always the true doctrine - just because it is new. This idea is not so much a form of modern thought as a form of modern lunacy. You cannot go home by walking very quickly in the opposite direction, and you are not of necessity nearing Land's End because you have just arrived at John o' Groat's. It is true that 'what we need is a fixed and absolute standard of values, that we may know what we want to get and where we want to go.' Without that, there can be no real progress. And yet it does seem to me that although that is evidently true, there is a certain amount of evidence to justify the belief that there is a Power greater than ourselves which goes on working its purpose out, *to a certain extent, over our heads as individuals and without our full knowledge and co-operation.* And the evidence for that I find mainly in that extraordinary historical crisis which is called the Industrial Revolution - the gift to man of mechanical power. What impresses me mainly about the Industrial Revolution is that it was the result of a gift from God, a pure and absolute 'bolt from the blue' so to speak. There seems to be no doubt that the enormous increase in productive power which has come to man in the last century and a half is the result in the main neither of capitalistic enterprise nor of manual labour, but of inventive genius, and inventive genius is a pure gift like poetry - you either have it or you haven't it, and if you haven't it you cannot get it; inventors are born, not made. And although it is not true that people who travel sixty miles an hour must be five times as civilised as people who travel only twelve, it is evident that the power of travelling sixty miles an hour or more, combined with the power of such rapid communication as is supplied by the telegraph, the telephone, and wireless, opens out entirely new possibilities for the world and the human race possibilities of union and of co-operation *which have never existed in the world before*. And these new possibilities do seem to have been worked out over our heads, and without our knowing whither we were being led. It is perfectly true that they do not in themselves constitute a progress in humanity, but they do provide for us a new and astounding opportunity for progress - true progress, with a perfectly definite and splendid objective which is the unity of the Human Race, the creation of Man, the great Human Brotherhood. That we are actually making any progress towards that objective is extremely difficult to prove. Nothing is more futile than attempted comparisons of this age with others that have preceded it. Anything can be proved by that method. People generally select out of one age what suits them and compare it with a selection from their own age made for the same reason, and then use the comparison to prove a pet theory which is really based much more upon their peculiar prejudice than upon any really rational grounds. That is very largely what the Dean does in his comparison between modern days and antiquity.

But as one surveys the whole drama of history it does seem to be enormously probable that Christ was right, and that the other name for that great Power which moves behind all things is Love, and that God is working out down the ages the purpose of Brotherhood. From our point of view He is working it out appallingly slowly and pain fully - it seems still to be miles and miles away. Those who have seen it, loved it, and longed for it, have received a dreadful setback in the last five years, in which the Human Brotherhood has been crucified and tortured. But even in the face of those hideous years a Christian can still believe, because the centre of his Faith is a Crucifix, behind which stands a tomb that is empty. He need not cut down his hopes for humanity at large to very modest and humble aspirations, as the Dean tells us we must do. He can believe that we have a millennium to look forward to, and that the Kingdom of God is at hand. The idea of progress in and through Christ is, I believe, the most powerful and man-moving reality in the world to-day, and I believe that we have in Christ a rational right to look upwards and onwards and to, see the New Jerusalem coming down from Heaven adorned as a bride for her husband. That is our objective.

G. A. STUDDERT KENNEDY.

ST. PAUL'S VICARAGE,
WORCESTER,
Jan. 6, 1921.

Contents

FOOD FOR THE FED-UP

I.   *Bread and Butter*

THE language that men spoke in France and Flanders was not always elegant, but it was always expressive. It was the speech of men who were up against realities, and it got there, and got there straight, wasting no time in plucking flowers of beauty by the way. Some of its expressions will live and some will die, perhaps some are better dead. One of its commonest phrases, whether it lives or dies, is a masterpiece of expressive diction, 'I'm fed up.' There is no English Dictionary equivalent for it. It expresses all the consciousness of waste and futility, all the bitterness of barren agony that men who lived in the valley of the shadow of death laughed at, because they could not afford to cry over it.

> 'Tain't the sufferin' as I grouse at,
>   I can stick my bit o' pain,
> But I keeps on allus askin',
>   What's the good and who's to gain?
> When you've got a plain objective
>   You can fight your fight and grin,
> But there ain't no damned objective,
>   And there ain't no prize to win.
> We're just like a lot o' bullocks
>   In a blarsted china shop,
> Bustin' all the world to blazes,
>   'Cause we dunno 'ow to stop,
> Trampling years of work and wonder
>   Into dust beneath our feet,
> And the one as does most damage
>   Swears that victory is sweet.'

The uselessness of life, the fatuous futility of our sufferings and pains, the boredom of energy expended to no purpose, and with no clear end in view, the pure silliness of modern warfare, is all summed up in those two words 'Fed up.' They express a state of mind which all good leaders knew to be the soldier's greatest enemy in war. An army of men who are fed up can have no hope of Victory, because they have no will to win. It is the soldier's greatest enemy in war, this state of mind, and the citizen's greatest enemy in time of peace. Men and women who are fed up can neither fight nor live. The dangers of the disease, and of the disasters that follow in its train, are greater in peace than they are in war, because the task of men in time of peace, the work they have to do, is so much more difficult and complicated than the simple work of war. The immediate purpose of war, at any rate, is clear: there is your enemy who will kill you if you do not kill him, and the consciousness of this simple purpose, this plain objective, with the tremendous motive-power of self-protection behind it, is enough to sustain energy and keep alive the will to work at most times. It was only in the intervals of what the Army, with a conscious or unconscious sense of humour, called 'Rest,' which meant endless marchings to and fro, and the forming of fours some thousands of times a day, it was only in those times that black doubts about the purpose and meaning of it all came down upon men like darkness, and weariness set in, and they groused, and were 'fed up.' Men who did not know the reason often said that the better off the soldier was, the farther he went back from the fighting line, the more he found to grouse at. Of course he did, because he had not then the saving sense of immediate purpose; if he was to keep going he had to find a larger purpose, and a more comprehensive meaning in it all, and that was hard to find - and often he did not find it, and was 'fed up.' But in time of peace there is no such clear immediate purpose, no 'plain objective' to sustain a man, beyond the purpose of living and the pleasures of life - and they are terribly apt to pall and grow monotonous. Doubts about the meaning and purpose of it all come knocking at the door. What's the use? Who's to gain? Why should one work, and work one's hardest, why should one do one's very best and put one's heart into life's work - what is it all for? Why should one give up anything or sacrifice anything, isn't it folly? Men work to live, and what is life but pleasure, enjoyment, and having a good time? Why should a man be unselfish? What is the good of self-sacrifice? Each man for himself, that is the common-sense policy, and the real gospel. It gets down to facts, and doesn't spout beautiful theories. And yet we know that, sensible as it sounds, that policy spells disaster pure and simple. Universal selfishness is another name for Hell on earth. Men can only live in peace together, building stable states and happy homes, at the cost of continual self-sacrifice. We know it deep down, but it is intensely hard to keep it always before us, this necessity of self-sacrifice. It is hard in any case, and impossible unless we have a clear vision of life's purpose, some plain and comprehensive objective. Where there is no open vision the people perish, they are bound to perish. There is no commanding motive for unselfishness wherewith to combat and overcome the immediate and pressing motives to self-seeking. Without some vision of life's purpose men fall back upon sensationalism and selfishness. They cannot help themselves. Like all other living things, men only move when they are tickled, so to speak, or, as the dignified psychologist would put it, all life is perpetual response to external stimuli, which sounds better in a book, but is really a comic way of saying the same thing. We only shift when we are tickled, and when there is nothing to tickle us into self-sacrifice we fall back on the selfish sensations that are always tickling us. That is what we have done. We are living for the sensation of the moment, and it is profoundly unsatisfying. It is like trying to live on fancy cakes - little bits of God knows what with cherries on top - pure sensations without satisfaction. You cannot live on them. You must have bread and butter, solid food; if you try a diet of fancy cakes you get fed up, which means you are still hungry, but can't eat. We have been trying it on. We have in these post-war days a sensational Press, a sensational stage, sensational dress, sensational literature, and sensational everything else, except sensational souls, and the consequence is that our daily lives are as dull as the daily press. They are full of murders, divorces, bloody massacres, and monotony. We are fed up. There is excuse for us. We have been tried as silver is tried, we have passed through fire and water and had a surfeit of self-sacrifice, we have given our best and bravest, and shed our blood in rivers, and we trusted that God would bring us out into a wealthy place, into a new world. But it is no new world that we find ourselves in, but an old world grown older, a world of selfishness grown more selfish, of greed that has grown more greedy, and of folly that knows no limit to its foolishness. There has come upon us a great disillusionment. We thought that the great Peace Conference was travailing to the birth of Peace, and it has brought forth an abortive pandemonium. Millions who gave up their all in a frenzy of self-sacrifice during the war are asking themselves bitterly what they gave it for. What's the good? and Who's to gain? We are fed up. It is dangerous, deadly dangerous, and must be cured - and there is only one cure for it. We must feed our souls on solid food, and not on the slops of sensationalism. We must regain our vision of life's purpose and set up a plain objective. We must, in fact, be able to repeat our Creed, and mean it - it is our first necessity.

We shall never know where we are politically, economically, or industrially until we know where we are religiously and morally. You cannot understand the part except upon some theory of the whole. You cannot be fixed about anything unless you have a faith about everything. We must have a creed.

And yet we are 'fed up' with creeds and formulas. We suspect them. What difference do they make? What does it matter what a man believes so long as he does what is right? Tell me something *you know* and I don't, and I'll listen to you, but as to what you believe, well, there is a shortage of paper and a surplus of hot air in the world already, don't add to it by writing a book about your creed. It is not your creed but your conduct I am concerned with. You can believe what you like - you can be a Roman Catholic or a Plymouth Brother, and in fact you can be a Calvinistic Confucian with leanings towards Buddhism if you like, so long as you pay your debts. Creeds don't count. It is doing right that matters. That is the common point of view. It sounds well, and is nonsense. It is all full of inaccuracies. It does not express thought, only feeling. It is doing right that matters. But what is Right? What ought we to do? What is our duty as men? A man does right when he fulfils the purpose of his life. But what is its purpose? An axe is a good axe when it cuts down trees - that is what it's for. A man is a good man when he does what? What is he for? Many things are right for one purpose that are all wrong for another. Many acts are right for a lower that are not right for higher purposes. Patriotism is right. It is right to love one's country. But 'Patriotism is not enough,' Nurse Cavell said before her death; 'we need to love our enemies.' Why do we need that? You cannot answer that question unless you have a creed. You cannot really answer any question involving right and wrong unless you have a creed, a belief about life's final purpose and the meaning of the world. A great many of the men directly responsible for this last Hell were acting rightly according to their conscience; they were acting patriotically, and that was enough according to their creed. They believed in God the Fatherland, Almighty Ruler of Heaven and Earth, and according to that creed their actions were right. Follow your conscience and you can't go wrong, is popular cant and claptrap. Many of the most damnable deeds in history were done by conscientious people. Their conscience was all right but their creed was all wrong. Your conscience is only an eye which must have light to see with, and your creed is the light by which your conscience sees. Without a creed it will trip you up and break your neck. On a pitch-black night all men are blind, and the man with keen eyes will often be the first to fall because he thinks he sees. A man can do a deadly wrong supposing it is right. The drunkard who treats his pal to drink and makes him like himself is doing unto others as he would they should do unto him, loving his neighbour as himself. He is acting out the golden rule apparently. But the golden rule is only gilt without a creed to guide it. Right conscience with a wrong creed will turn the human race into a herd of swine helping one another to wallow on a muck-heap. When you talk about doing right without a creed you may sound sensible, but you are really talking straight through the middle of your Sunday hat.

All men act upon their real creed. It may not be the creed that they profess, because they may be liars or hypocrites - most men are both more or less - it may not be the creed that they profess, but it must inevitably be the creed that they believe, from which men's normal actions spring. When you stop talking and start thinking, you are bound to come to it. The only thing that really does matter is what god a man worships and believes in.

You must have a god or gods. Your god is what you live for, and you must live for something, if it is only your dinner. If you live for your dinner, then your god is your belly, and a very common god too. A real atheist would not need to commit suicide, he would be dead already. He would be like old soldiers, he would not die, but simply fade away. If you live, you must live for something, and what you live for is your god, and your actions are based upon your belief that it is what you ought to live for - your real creed. The drunkard's real creed is, 'I believe in Alcohol Almighty, Lord of all good living, bestower of True Peace. I believe in the fiery Spirit that can give the coward courage and make the dumb man speak, that soothes all sorrows, dries all tears, and gives the weary rest.' That is his real creed, and his actions are based upon it, in fact his nose is coloured by it.

The most popular creed is still the one with which the human race began - the belief in many gods. Men are naturally polytheists. They tend to believe in and worship anything that touches them, grips them, possesses them, and lifts them out of themselves. Men have destroyed the temples of Bacchus, but they worship the Wine God still; they have thrown down the shrines of Venus, but millions believe in Lust; they have broken the images of Mars, but still his hoarse voice calls the nations out to slay, and his fever - War Fever - turns men into beasts. Christ has won the churches, but the old gods hold the streets. Many a man who professes the fashionable belief in one God does not believe in that God at all, but in half a dozen different idols that seem to give him what he needs.

The average man is still a polytheist, and as long as you remain a worshipper of many gods you will remain an average man, you will run with the ruck, doing what other people do, saying what other people say, and thinking what other people think, bitten with every passing craze, from diabolo to barbaric dances, priding yourself on your sanity because you are as mad as all the other lunies. You will be a sort of person, but no sort of a personality. You will not be able to say with any truth, 'I believe,' not merely because you have no belief, but because you have no 'I' to believe with. You won't have a real 'Ego,' you will be a split personality, a house divided against itself, with Dr. Jekyll in the dining-room, Mr. Hyde in the kitchen, and God knows who stowed away in the basement. You will not be able to rely upon yourself, because you won't have a self to rely on, only a mob of selves clamouring for satisfaction.

The fundamental difficulty of making peace on earth is that we cannot find enough men of goodwill - in fact, we cannot find enough men of any will at all, good or bad. We strive to make a united world out of divided people, divided not merely from one another, but divided within themselves. St. James was in the right when he said, 'Why are there wars and battles among you? Isn't it because there is a conflict of passions within you? You are eaten up with desires and find no satisfaction. You butcher your brothers and get up agitations, and they land you nowhere. You plunge the world into battles and great wars, but don't get what you want because you won't pray, or if you do, your prayers are rotten ones, because you only want food to squander on your lusts.' That is the root of the matter. We talk in splendid bombast about the 'Will of the People,' but God alone knows where to find it, or what it is. The job is to find a man with a 'Will,' let alone a people. Most men don't know what they want, and won't be happy till they get it. And there can be no peace for men in that condition. The first step toward peace is to kill polytheism and convert the world to the worship of one God. You cannot unite men with one another who are divided within themselves. The first necessity is the concentration of your Faith which is another name for your life-force upon one God, one goal, one governing purpose. If you can accomplish that concentration or surrender, you will become, or be on the road to becoming, a personality, a character. You may, of course, become a bad character - that will depend upon what god you choose. If you take a low god you will be a character, but a low character. If you take money, for instance, and make it your one god, if you live for it, work for it, give up everything else and follow it, you will become a distinct person - in fact, you may become a profiteer, and a member of Parliament or a peer. Almost any god will give you for a while the power and joy of monotheism, and that is the very essence of all real power and joy. The joy of the monotheist is what all the world, consciously or unconsciously, is seeking. No man knows the meaning of pure joy until he can say with complete conviction, 'I have found it, I believe in one god.' The joy of the lover for whom all the world grows golden because his mistress smiles, the joy of the artist absorbed in his dream of beauty, form and colour, the joy of the musician drunk with his million melodies, all these are the joys of the monotheist - they are the ecstasies of the man who has found the one thing which is for him supremely well worth while, and has surrendered himself utterly into its service. That is the essence of bliss, and for a while almost any old god will do it for you; men have got it out of whole-hearted devotion to anything - from bottling bugs to badminton, and from serving Christ to playing poker. For a while any one god will do. But only for a while. It won't last. You have a many-sided nature, and you can fool part of your nature all the time, and the whole of your nature part of the time, but you cannot fool all your nature all the time. Sooner or later, if your one god is not big enough, and true enough, part of your nature will rebel, and turn rotten on you - and you will be 'fed up' again. If you would have the joy of the monotheist as a lasting thing, you must not only find your one god, but that god must be big enough and true enough to satisfy the whole of your nature, or to give such clear promise of final satisfaction as will keep you seeking. The worship of idols is like the taking of drugs, it ends in desperation. That is why so many great souls have been supremely unhappy in love. They sought, as all men seek, the one God, and for a moment thought they saw him shining in some poor woman's eyes, and, of course, fell down and worshipped, and asked their goddess to ascend God's throne and be the ruler of the stars. Then when she proved unfitted for that job, and took to bearing babies as a human substitute, they turned in disgust and left her. All the love poetry of the world, which the materialist in his fatuous wisdom ascribes to the 'sex instinct,' is written just as really in praise of

God as the hymn of any saint. The golden joy that thrills through it and reveals a wonder world is just a faint and distant shadow of the joy and beauty that will transform the earth when men have really done with idols and can say their Creed in truth.

The instinct of the world is right in rejecting purely formal creeds and dogmas as of no importance. Of course they are of no importance. Purely formal anythings are of no importance. Purely formal five-pound notes would be of no importance. But real five-pound notes are of great importance. They may mean health, and strength, and music, and art, and poetry, and love, and children, and laughter, and mountains, and sea, and sunshine, and heaven or hell - they mean life or death. To throw out the reality because the form is in itself of no importance, is pouring out the baby with the bathwater. Of course the form is in itself of no importance, and while creeds are only forms they are purely silly. But creeds must have a form - like everything else in this odd world. They must find expression somehow. Like every other spiritual thing, they must have a material symbol of some sort. That is the best name ever given to creeds, and it is a pity we did not stick to it. They are 'symbols' of Truth. Symbols, mind you, not exhaustive statements. There isn't such a thing existing as an exhaustive statement of final Truth. We don't know it yet, and therefore cannot state it. The creeds are no more complete statements of truth than a soldier's love-letter from the front was a complete statement of his love. You know the kind of letter. 'My dear Eliza, - I hope this finds you in the pink, as it leaves me at present. I hope to come on leave soon. Roll on Peace. Mind you don't forget me. With love and kisses, your affectionate Bill.' And then as many crosses as the paper would permit. This is not an expression of reality - it is ridiculous as an expression, but it was to Eliza enormously satisfying as a symbol. She slept on it, lived with it - it was life, and love, and laughter, and sun, moon, and stars, and that is what creeds and dogmas are - ridiculous as expressions, but wonderful as symbols. All dogmas are poetry, and can only be understood and criticised as poetry as an endeavour to symbolise what cannot be stated. To treat creeds as you would treat scientific statements of observed fact is like reading Keats as you would an order for Keating's Powder. The brevity of the form is deceptive. It is taken as the brevity of careful prose, when it really is the brevity of lyric poetry. You know what I mean. Poetry does not say what it means, it hints at it. So do creeds. They are absurd as statements, but superb as symbols. You must have them - you must have dogmas. Undogmatic teaching is the driest, dullest, dreariest thing in the world. It is teaching minus conviction - brief, bright, and breezy talks to the people on popular subjects that pass the time away and get nowhere. O my holy Aunt, how fed up one gets with that business! It only consists in dressing up platitudes and putting powder on their noses to make them presentable. Undogmatic teaching is so broad-minded that it is not deep enough to wet the uppers of your boots. It gets nowhere. It has no god. It tells men to worship all the gods in moderation, and not to go too far with any of them, because of God, the great policeman, who has a big stick to beat any one who goes the whole hog about anything. Undogmatic teaching can't be Christian, because it has to be careful - it must not hurt any one's feelings, so anything is as true as anything else; it is all a matter of opinion - nobody really knows - you just believe what you like; it is just disguised agnosticism, and that is the dullest and most cowardly of all creeds. You must have dogmas, because you can't have convictions without symbols to express them, and you must have convictions because you must have a God; it all comes back to that. What we need is not less dogma, but more of it - tons of it. Only it must be dogma properly understood. Dogma is the potted poetry of faith. It is the radium of reality. Don't let's talk any more nonsense about abolishing creeds; you might as well try to abolish bread and butter. Let us find out what our creed is, and whether it reveals to us a God to whom we can surrender ourselves, body, soul, and spirit.

If our creed is only a form, that may be our fault, not the creed's. You can bet on this - *You don't really believe your creed until you want to say it standing at spiritual attention with the roll of drums in your ears, the light of love dazzling your eyes, and all the music of a splendid world crashing out a prelude to its truth.* If your creed is dull, it is dead, or you are dead, and either one or the other of you must be made alive again. Either you must change your creed, or your creed must change you. That is the problem that faces us - are we to change the Christian creed, or is the Christian creed to change us? I'm betting on the creed every time, and I want to tell you why.

II.   *I believe in God the Father*

WE must have a creed, a symbol of our faith in this world's final meaning and purpose, or we shall become 'fed up' with life. I don't believe that there exists, or could exist, a much better creed than that which we call the Apostles' Creed. If a man can lay hold on its inner meaning - if he can see the truth it hints at, however dimly - I believe he is on his way to find the great Reality to which he can dedicate every power he possesses, and in which he can find satisfaction for every fine desire of his soul. It is a wonderful little document. It blazes with colour, radiates romance, and stirs the blood like a battle cry. It only needs that we should wipe the dust of ages from our eyes, and see behind its short sharp sentences the Light which gave it birth, and it becomes a living creed for living men. It flings out its challenge abruptly. It does not argue, it challenges an argument. It does not do your thinking for you, it calls you out to think, and act, and love, and pray.

To me it is always preceded by a flourish of trumpets. It shouts out its great guess at final reality, and calls upon brave men to stake their lives upon its truth. It recognises that life is a great gamble. There are no final certainties, only tremendous probabilities. If you will not gamble in this life, then you cannot live, you can only linger. That is why the gambling instinct in human nature is almost as strong as life itself. That is why the effort to kill it is bound to be a failure. Some of the finest flowers of human history sprang from that instinct as their seed. It is the spirit of enterprise, adventure, courage - the very pith and core of manhood. Of course you only play with and degrade it when you merely put money on a contest of horses. Life calls you to bet your heart-strings on a conflict of gigantic forces. Saying your creed is booking your bet, your bet of body, mind, and spirit, on a great chance. You are right if you seek to understand the chance and count the odds up carefully, but you are wrong if you refuse to bet because you can't be sure. Taking risks is the only way to safety. The man who will not bet is the genuine agnostic, and a really genuine agnostic can never know what life is. He could not marry because his wife might play him false, and would not dare to have a child because it might be born cross-eyed. Whatever power there is behind this world, it must have a sporting element in it, because it has no use for men who will not take risks. The great creed recognises that, and calls on men to bet on a great tip.

Is the world good or bad? That is the question. Is it good or evil? That life at present is a contest between the two is not a question but a certainty. Here they are, good and evil, at it hammer and tongs under our very noses. Life calls out to us, 'Roll up, roll up, to the great fight. What's the betting, Black or White? pay your money and take your choice.' To that challenge the creed replies, 'I back White - back it all out - my last shirt, and my only pair of breeches.' 'I believe in God the Father Almighty, Maker of Heaven and Earth.' Good is finally Almighty, Evil hasn't a dog's chance. That is the Christian bet, which a man books when he stands to say the Apostles' Creed.

That is the root meaning of the first clause. The Christian is an Optimist, and believes that at its heart the world is good. It is well to get that fixed for a start, because there are those who reject Christianity to-day as being a pessimistic faith, and they have some reason on their side. In a book of his called *The New Optimism,* Mr. H. de Vere Stacpoole says, 'Nothing satisfies me but the faith I have struck out for myself, and the philosophy that a child can understand. And that faith is simply in the essential goodness of the world. .. Christianity believes in the essential badness of the world. .. All men are sinners. .. Christianity believes that the world is bad to the core, and yet believes that a God who is all goodness made man all at once, and thoroughly bad; left him in that condition for an indefinite time, and then sent His Son down to redeem him.'

Now I am sure he is wrong; I am sure that the plain Christian Creed has never been pessimistic. These brave words: 'I believe in God the Father Almighty, Maker of Heaven and Earth,' shout out defiance of pessimism. Yet it cannot be denied that theologians have so misinterpreted and twisted the meaning of the great challenge that it has appeared as if men were really called upon to believe in just that blasphemous absurdity from which he turns - the pessimistic lie that this world is bone bad, and that the most we can expect is that God will save a remnant of its teeming millions from a lost and ruined universe, and that all the rest must be cast for ever into the eternal furnace where their worm dieth not and the fire is not quenched. It cannot be denied that any amount of Christian theology and philosophy is based upon that idea. The whole cycle of doctrines that surround the 'Fall of Man,' 'Original Sin,'"Eternal Punishment,' 'Propitiation,' and the 'Sacrifice of the Cross,' have been, and still are, so stated as to give the impression, not indeed that God made the world bone bad - Mr. Stacpoole goes too far there - but that at some point in time the world that God made good met with an awful disaster and fell under a curse which turned it from a garden of glorious flowers into a wilderness of weeds, from which man was doomed to wring subsistence by the toil of his hands and the sweat of his brow, and in that awful state it remained until Christ came with His offer of salvation for those who would accept. And, moreover, even this offer has been made to mean not that He came to retrieve the ruin of the world, but to save the elect from that hopeless ruin and preserve them for life in the world to come. Salvation was put off until after death. This world of sunshine, sea, and flowers remained a splendid ruin - the monument of a past without a future.

That has been the idea behind a tremendous amount of Christian teaching; it is pessimistic, and I feel, with Mr. Stacpoole, that it is blasphemous and absurd.

Christian theology has been, and is still often ghastly wrong, but what I maintain is that the Christian religion, the intuitive faith which is the fire behind its creeds, has always been supremely right. It has never believed that matter or the material world were essentially bad. It has bidden men learn of the lilies, and find their God through bread and wine. It has bidden us give thanks for this world's goods, and blessed the labour of our hands. It has always been a sacramental religion, calling us to find God in the world, and through it, and has stuck like glue to the faith that the 'Maker of Heaven and Earth' was Almighty Good. It has always been optimistic.

But what about all this pessimistic business? Well, you know optimism isn't easy. Easy optimism is tomfoolery. Any optimism which does not face the fact of evil is just a blind fool's paradise built upon shifting sands. It is no good trying to explain evil away; it is a flaming fact. Easy optimism turns you sick. We have too much of it. That is the root error of much of the socialistic teaching. Evil - lust, spite, envy, pride, hatred - is not really faced, and their splendid theories of the perfect social system are just wild dreams, because they are based upon the easy optimistic lie that there is no evil to be faced; it can all be organised, legislated, and educated away. Men are only the angel victims of a corrupt oligarchy and a pernicious social system. But that is pure tomfoolery; any man who honestly reads his own heart knows that. Evil is a stubborn fact of human nature, and no scheme is any real good which does not provide a remedy for it, and no optimism is sound at all which does not take it into count. Trying to persuade sane men that all the blackguards live in Park Lane, and all the saints in Whitechapel, is just as much pure foolery with facts as the endeavour to turn it the other way round. And, moreover, the natural world is not an altogether beautiful or perfect thing; it is full of cruelties and crudities, and is apparently utterly indifferent to matters of right and wrong. There is no need to lard it on, is there? It is a queer business. It looks as if the only thing to do was to leave it - give it up as hopeless. But that sooner or later spells pessimism, disguise it how you may. You have to get down to it. *Well, the Christian teachers did get down to it;* that is to their credit. They had to justify their religious optimism, their belief that at its heart the world was good - philosophically and theologically facing the fact of evil. Their efforts to do it produced queer results - results which often looked like blank pessimism, but never were in the inner meaning pessimistic - only honest. Their faith was always right; their theology was inevitably often wrong. Their scheme of things is to us now blankly incredible. The scheme of Salvation, which starts in the Garden of Eden and ends before the great White Throne, seems like a fairy tale to us, and not a very moral one at that. It does not satisfy us a scrap, and there is no use pretending that it does. We simply can't believe in this utter disaster that came upon the world - in the Fall, the Flood, the Ransom paid to the Powers of Evil, and the propitiation of God's just wrath. It lies right outside reality for most of us, and there is no good tinkering with it. It is all an effort to face facts with such knowledge as its authors had at their command, and it is impossible for us to bring ourselves back into the atmosphere of their minds. We can't do it. Why? What change has come over us? Well, the fact of the matter is, that there has been born to us an idea, not a really new idea, but an idea which has been coming to birth all down the ages, and with which the mind of man has been travailing for centuries. It is the idea of Progress. Whether or not the world is now progressing is a very debatable question, and it certainly is impossible to prove to demonstration that it is. But that is not the real point. The real point is that it has become impossible for us to think of the world except in terms of motion, just as impossible as it is to think of it except in terms of cause and effect. The idea of motion - movement - has taken hold of us, gripped us, and we cannot get away from it, and we have an intuitive conviction that it is vitally important. It may in time prove to be an inadequate idea, but we are convinced that it will never be proved to be a false idea. It has got into our very blood and bones, and, of course, it has got into our religion. In spite of tremendous efforts to keep it out, it has become perfectly plain that either we must admit it, and interpret God - the Christian God - in terms of progress and movement, or else force people to find a new god. So powerful is the idea that it can, and has, become an idol, and men have fallen down and worshipped progress, and surrendered themselves to it with all the fervour of the true monotheist. For the space of many years there has been a great crowd shouting, 'Great is Evolution of the Scientists.' It has given men for a while greater comfort and stronger courage than the Saviour Christ; it has restored their confidence in the future, filled them with hope, and been the Father of some burning charity. It has been the battle-cry of a wonderful army of devoted workers for social justice and scientific truth. It has for many taken the place of God Himself, and bowed Him calmly out of His Own Universe. It is of no avail for men to write books to show that the idea is largely an assumption - a pure hypothesis. It may be, but it has proved such an inspiring and fruitful hypothesis, that men simply cannot afford to give it up except for something nobler and better, and that is not forthcoming. The alternative that Christian theology offers hasn't a dog's chance. Christian theology of the orthodox sort - that is the sort that clings not merely to the spirit, but to the letter of the Church's formularies - is all couched in terms of Providence - Static and Stable Providence. God is conceived of in terms of absolute Monarchy. He is the Great King Who administers justice, and maintains order in a static finished world, distributes His favours to whom He pleases, ordaining the lives of men according to His Will. He is the God of battles, Who declares War and maintains Peace. Whatever happens is the result of His command. He has endless forces at His call to coerce men to obedience. Plague, pestilence, famine, disease, and sudden death in a thousand forms are the weapons that He wields. He made this earth as a training ground for a future life, and at His pleasure He will destroy it, fill up the number of His elect, hold the great Assize, damn all rebels to Hell, and reign supreme in Heaven. It is all worked out in metaphors belonging to another age and another political system. Men thought in those days in terms of Providence and Security; we think in terms of Progress and Adventure. They thought in terms of Despotism, and we think in terms of Democracy and Self-Government. It is not so much that this presentation is untrue to us, it is worse; it is unreal, it is chimerical, it is the stuff that dreams are made of, and romances of a bygone day. It is like a love story of the time of Alfred the Great, vaguely interesting, but not convincing. We cannot get there. It is all static. This world is finished, complete, and the only change we have to contemplate is the change from this world to another. To us this world is moving, growing; it is not finished, it is on a journey; it is part of something much larger than itself, which is all changing, all growing, with a growth in which we all share. We cannot get away from this idea of growth; it is in the very air we breathe, and it was not in the air our fathers breathed; they never really grasped it at all.

That is the change. The point we have to think on is this. Does this idea mean that we must abandon the old Creed, abandon Christ as the Saviour of the World, or can we interpret the Creed in terms of the great idea? I believe we can and must. I believe that the new idea comes from God, that it is new light which brings out the essential meaning of Christ's teaching much more fairly and fully than the old could ever do. It lights up this whole question of evil and of good.

The world is moving; every soul is moving, growing - where to? that is the essential point to decide. It is the essential point about every movement - where is it going to end? What is its tendency? If the world is a movement, the question as between optimism or pessimism is different. We do not ask, is the world good or bad? but is it growing better or growing worse? What is its tendency? The scientists lead us wrong in one way while they poured light upon us in others. They lead us wrong because they fixed our attention upon where the world had come from; they turned our minds backwards, and kept them gazing into the past. That is not good, nor is it a true way of looking at a movement. The only point in looking back at all is that you may learn to look forward. That is what we can do. If we take a good look backwards, and get the picture there displayed well into our minds, then we can look forward in the right direction. Now when you do look back in the light of the new knowledge, it is a strange picture that you see. There was a time when there was no life on this planet at all. There was a time when it could not have supported life, when it was probably nothing but incandescent vapour slowly cooling. I am not sure that the preparation for what we call life, is not more wonderful, more utterly bewildering, than the growth of life itself. When one contemplates the complicated network of conditions that must have been provided and made continual before anything could live, the idea that these conditions were brought about by chance or accident seems ridiculous. To watch with the eyes of imagination, backed with knowledge, this strange amorphous thing changing and forming itself into a fit home for life, beats all the wonder of the Creation story of Genesis into a cocked hat, and, moreover, it is a wonder that grips us now; it is based on fact and not on fable; it has left its story written in the material of which the world is made, and it puts all pride of man, and all impertinent pretensions on our part, out of court. If a great scientist succeeded in discovering the origin of life and making a living thing, what would it mean? Why merely that this tremendous process had produced a being of such perfect intelligence that he could actually reproduce, with all the previous conditions provided, the first and smallest miracle that was originally performed by the process itself without any visible agent to perform it at all. It would not abate the wonder of the Creation one whit. I repeat that the preparation of the world for life is more staggering than the coming of life itself. Once get the wonder of that preparation through your head, and you will be ready for anything, and will be incapable of regarding the world as a thing devoid of meaning. *It must have been meant for life.*

Then through the movement life breaks. Its origin is a mystery, and must remain one no matter what is discovered. It was the result of the process. Another drama starts on the previously constructed stage - the drama of life itself. It is a strange and tragic story. It is full of cruelty and apparently purposeless waste. Life takes the weirdest forms. Weird growths of every sort without any apparent use or meaning. Awful reptiles and savage beasts, all teeth and belly and claws, wallowing in fetid swamps, and gorging themselves on other living things. Sitting up and blinking with bleered eyes at a blazing sun, as they lick blood from their slimy jaws. This kind of ghastly shambles, without a gleam of intelligence, or a trace of gentleness, goes on for thousands of years. If you could have lived then, you would have said that the world was a ghastly joke made by some gigantic Being with the mind of a Chinese torturer. But they that live longest see most, and through the peepholes supplied by fossils and rocks we can watch the drama proceed. Gradually there comes into its action a new element, the element of intelligence, and we soon perceive that this is a power that is going to challenge physical strength. The smaller and more intelligent animals survive the gigantic monsters. They adapt themselves more readily, secure food more easily, move more quickly. They look much weaker, but are much stronger. It is the beginning of the great paradox of life whereby weakness proves stronger than strength. Already the Power behind life is beginning to put down the mighty from their seats and exalt the humble and meek. Already mind is overcoming matter. Then out of the twilight peers the face of the first man. He is one of the smaller animals, and not much different from them except for a light in his eyes that seems to promise greater intelligence. Had you been living then, I imagine it might have struck you for a moment that there was an intelligent look in that ape's face, and then you would have forgotten it. He was only a freak perhaps, and not so much different from the others after all. But that is where you would have been wrong. That gleam is to grow into a blazing sun; it is to change the whole appearance of the world; it is to build cities, paint pictures, make music, tame lightning; it is to make the whole earth servant to its will. These little differences in living things want watching; you can't tell what they mean. The whole history of man sprang from that gleam in his eye as the ape swung up into his tree to rest. Look back along that history. Watch the development of the peculiarly human powers, and see if you can guess at what they mean. Speech the animals had, but man developed it almost beyond recognition. Then he added to it writing. They both aided him in his struggle to survive. He has added music, painting, then later printing, telegraphy, telephony, wireless communication, etc. What do they all mean? The simplest of them is enormously complicated. The gift of speech - the disturbance of the atmosphere by wagging the bit of meat inside your jaws and flopping it against your teeth, thus setting up vibration which beats on your companion's ear-drum, sets the nerves quivering and travels to his brain, and then by the sudden and dramatic leap which no living being understands (except that they might tell you that it was due to the working of 'invariably concomitant psycho-physical parallelism' - and if that helps you, you are welcome to it), he gets ideas in his mind similar to the ideas that are passing through yours - it's a bewildering business; and when you add to it the gift I am now exercising, sitting in a chair with a copying ink pencil - a bit of a tree with some odd material in it that makes marks on some wood-pulp or rags - and making thousands of strange signs and symbols which will be taken up by a man who will translate their meaning and put up similar signs made of lead in a vast machine, and then stamp the signs some thousands of times on to more wood-pulp and rags, and produce that mystery of mysteries, a Book, and proceed to sell it to some man I never saw in my life; some one perhaps sitting up in San Francisco, who will take it up and drink in through his eyes the ideas that are coming from God knows where into my mind, as I sit here in a silent study thousands of miles away. Good Lord, but a book is a queer thing when you come to think of it, isn't it? So is a piece of music. Beethoven sits up deaf as a doorpost, and the music of the Moonlight Sonata sings itself into his head. He takes woodpulp and some black liquid and a bit of steel, and makes blobs and lines, and scratches on it. He dies, gets buried, and my friend comes into the drawing-room and sits down at a big lump of wood with some wires and hammers inside; he pulls out a music book, looks at it, beats the notes that work the hammers, and there floats out upon the air the same stream of delicious sounds that sang themselves in the brain of Beethoven, and I sit here and see again, through the old musician's eyes, the moonlight on still water shining, and hear the rippling of a little stream, and feel the touch of summer air, soft velvet like a woman's cheek - and Beethoven is dead - and, O my holy aunt! it is a queer business, isn't it? What does it mean? It is all the result of the weird process that began with incandescent vapour and monstrous pterodactyles licking bloody chops beside a slimy swamp. And it's a thoroughly nasty process, it's a bloody and a cruel process, it's a wasteful and non-moral process, and it is an every other sort of adjective you can imagine in the dictionary and out of it process; and yet it issues in the music of Beethoven and the Life of Jesus Christ, and in these strange gifts that baffle and bewilder one to think about.

What is one to make of it? Well, there is one thing stands out: all these peculiarly human gifts have one result; they enable men to unite, to co-operate, to share a common fund of knowledge, of Truth and Beauty. They break down our isolation from one another and draw us into a closer unity. They tend to make men, millions of men, into Man - the Race, the Human Unity. They are means of increasing Love. There is not a single peculiarly human gift that has not got that tendency; they all tend to make unity possible; they all tend towards Love. I look backward, and though my eyes are often blurred with tears, and I grow hot with anger, still I seem to see a meaning struggling through it all, and it is best expressed in the word Love. That is what the process seems to be groping towards - the Brotherhood of Man in Love. That is what it does seem to be moving to, but under whose guidance? By what power? By accident? Go on. By necessity? I don't know what that means. There must be something behind it as big as that which has come and is coming out of it - as big as Man, with a capital M. There must be some one behind it who has in him the Brotherhood of Man. God the Father? Yes, that does it. I come back to it when I have viewed the process. I am driven to discover behind it God the Father - a power that means the Brotherhood of Man, and has it in His Heart. Mind you, I hate the process. I think it's loathsome. But I can't do Mr. H. G. Wells's touch, and beat my breast, and say the only God I have is the Undying Fire within my soul. I know that I came out of the process - Undying Fire and all; I am the product of it, the child of it; and though I may not like my parents' looks, I can't disown it, since it issued in me. I must have been in it, I and all the noblest of my kind must have been in it - Jesus Christ, St. Francis of Assisi, the most blazing furnaces of Undying Fires - they must all have been in it, or rather in the Power behind it. I cannot separate myself from it, and set myself over against it as an enemy. A man can't fight his own father; that is just it. We are coming to it - my own Father, our own Father. He must be behind it. There is in me - there was in the best of my race - a longing for this Brotherhood of Man, and it must be in the Process or Power behind it. He must be - Our Father, Maker of Heaven and Earth - the Author of the Process. Do I believe in Him? Well, He has done a lot. He has produced the longing for Brotherhood and the means of making it. Do I believe in Him? Will I bet on His success? It seems sensible, and besides, there is something calling, something deep down inside. It's a bloody process, as bloody and unbeautiful as a Cross, but it has done a lot. I do feel like betting on the Future. Yes, I believe in God the Father. Almighty? I don't know. What does that mean?

III.   *Almighty?*

WEhave reached this point. The process by which this world has come to be what it is must have some one behind it. He may be more than a person, and He can't be less. He appears to be a Being Who has within Himself not merely persons but a unity of persons, a sort of Brotherhood. That is what appears to be working its way out through the process, so I suppose it must be in the final cause of it. I am driven to that conclusion. You see, we must look at the movement in the light of its latest results; that is the only way in which we can rightly judge any movement. We must look at nature in the light of human nature, and the best human nature. We cannot look at it apart from ourselves. Trying to understand nature apart from man is like trying to understand a body without a head, which is a hopeless job. We have suffered from that sort of nonsense. When writers talk of nature they very often don't make it clear what they mean, but if it is to have any real meaning, it must mean the whole universe, the whole show complete. You cannot divide it up. It is a universe. Cabbages are no more natural than kings, and Julius Caesar was just as natural as a jelly-fish. It is a unity, and a single movement, and we must judge it in the light of its latest results; and when we consider its latest result, viz. 'Men,' and ask ourselves the meaning of their peculiarly human powers - speech, writing, art, music, printing, mechanical invention, telegraphy, telephony, wireless communication, etc. - they all seem to have one tendency, they seem to make for unity, they are all means to unity, to the Creation of Man - the united human race. That purpose is not accomplished, it is not nearly accomplished, but it looks as if it was being accomplished. And the queer part of it is that it seems as if it was being accomplished without our individually fully comprehending what the purpose is. It is as though, to spite our stupidity and selfishness, some great Power were working a purpose out, moulding our blind and selfish efforts to His Will. Under the guidance of this Power we appear to be blundering on towards brotherhood. The almost dramatic discovery of mechanical power in the last century gives one that impression very strongly. No one, I suppose, has contributed more to the Creation of Man than the builders of railways and inventors of more rapid means of communication, yet one doubts if they knew what they were doing in the least. Their powers of invention were gifts. If any one can be said to be inspired it is an inventor. Inventive power is as much a gift as music or poetry or pink eyes; you don't earn it and you can't force it, it just comes from God knows where - only He must know. The gift comes and makes things for their own sake, or for the sake of money or a woman's love, or just for fun, because it can't help itself. And it is only after ages that the purpose of all the gifts becomes apparent at all - the final purpose. So one gets the sense of a superior Power or Intelligence gradually working out a colossal idea - the idea of Human Brotherhood and Unity - the Creation of Man. What infinite purpose that is part of we cannot comprehend, but it probably is part of a larger scheme, because this earth is only a speck in an infinite universe. A survey of the process forces in upon the mind that sense of some one turning much more out of our actions than we can understand or foresee. We co-operate half blindfold, and almost without any conscious desire to do so. The Creation of Man seems a thousand times more possible to-day than it did two centuries ago, and we can hardly say that we have consciously tried to make it so. As then, this purpose of human brotherhood seems to have been working itself out through the process all the time, and as it seems vastly improbable that it can be doing so by an infinite series of accidents, we come to the conclusion that there must be some one behind it, who must at least be a person, and is probably more, and if we are to give Him a name, it is difficult to see what better name we could give Him than' Father,' not merely because He produced us, but also because it is apparently His purpose and plan to make a family of us. He has done a great deal towards it, and it looks as if He was going to do more, and I am drawn very strongly to back Him, to believe in Him, to bet my life upon Him and His plan. So I come to say in a very real sense, 'I believe in God the Father, Maker of Heaven and Earth,' Author of the Process. But this Creed of ours goes further and adds the word 'Almighty.' Now at that word I am inclined to bogle and hesitate. What does it mean? And my hesitation grows greater when I am told that absolute sovereign power is an essential attribute of God, that He can know no let or hindrance to the working of His Will, that He is absolute Master in His own universe, and all things move in obedience to His command. It seems, then, that I am required to believe that every detail of this process is the direct result of His Will, and is good. Now that is what I cannot do. The process seems to me to be a cruel and a bloody business. I cannot say that war, disease, pestilence, famine, and all the other characteristics of the process are good. If this word 'Almighty' means that the Father could have made this world, and obtained the results He desires, in a thousand other ways, but that He deliberately chose this, that makes my gorge rise. Why in thunder choose this one? It is disreputable if He could have done it otherwise, without this cruelty and wrong. It is not commonly respectable. He must be an evil-minded blackguard, with a nasty disposition like a boy that likes pulling the wings off flies. I cannot get up any reverence for such a being. Why, bless my life, He tortures children, voluntarily tortures them to death, and has done so for thousands of years. I can't stand that at all - it's dirty; and when I am told that I must believe it, and that every detail of the process was planned and carried out precisely as He wished, I begin to turn sick. Snakes, sharks, and blood-sucking vermin - what sort of a God is this? He chose this way because He gloried in it! That beats the band. It turns me clean against the process. I cannot see its beauty for its brutality. I cannot hear the lark sing for the squealing of a rabbit tortured by a stoat, I cannot see the flowers for the face of a consumptive child with rotten teeth, the song of the saints is drowned by the groans of murdered men. *Nothing can justify this method of Creation but absolute Necessity.* This way is only tolerable if it is *the only way.* There must be a great necessity binding upon the Creator. He must have taken this way because there was no other way to take. He must hate the process if He is good just as much as I do, and more, and I do hate it with all my heart. And yet I cannot adopt the dignified defiance attitude, and set myself up in judgment of it, refusing to recognise any God but the still small voice within my soul. I can't do that because it is not honest. I couldn't have a soul or a still small voice or a mind or anything else apart from the process; I am the product of it, I am part of it, one with it. I am one with all life, one with earth and sky and sea, one with birds and beasts and fishes. I kill them, eat them, prey on them, but love them still. I cannot separate myself from nature, or nature from myself. I cannot simply defy the process, still less can I wholly assent or submit to it. I must somehow come to terms with it, find a Friend through it, but He must be better than the process is. He must be beyond as well as in it - morally beyond it - or He can be no Friend of mine. He must be as good as I am; my inmost being demands that, and my intelligence demands it because He produced me, and I am better than the process. If that sounds arrogant I can't help it; I've got to cling fast to the best that is in me, or suffer shipwreck. That is the very disaster that has befallen many souls; they degraded themselves by submitting to a Will of God which in their best moments they knew to be immoral, and by bowing their heads when they should have fought. I must not do it, nor must you. In a world like this you cannot respect yourself unless you are a rebel; every decent man must be a rebel. What I want to be is a rebel in the name of God. But if God is 'Almighty God, King of all Kings, and Governor of all things, whose Power no creature is able to resist' - as the Prayer Book puts it - how can I help making Him absolutely responsible for every detail of the process, and assuming that every happening in it is the result of His Will action on it? The conclusion seems inevitable. Yet what grounds have we for believing that there exists, or can exist, this 'Sovereign power of Good that knows no let or hindrance to the working of His Will?' What grounds have we for believing that God is a Being whose Power no creature is able to resist? As far as I can see, there is no evidence for it whatever, and an enormous weight of evidence against it. I cannot find in heaven or earth a trace of the existence of such a Power. But men say you degrade God if you make His Power less than absolute. If His Power is not absolute, if He is not complete Master in His own universe, then He is not perfect. But who says so? Whose idea of perfection is that? Why must perfection of necessity include the possession of what we call absolute power? What right have we to assert that there is or can be such a thing in existence at all? What does 'Being Master in His own universe' mean? It seems to be an essentially human metaphor, drawn from our own experience by a negative process, and arising from our chronic disposition to confuse Power with Force. This feeling that God's perfection demands that He should be possessed of power as complete as that of a potter over a piece of clay seems to be the result of thinking that God's ways are our ways, and of making God in man's image in the wrong sense. We try to protect God's dignity as though, like the dignity of our earthly kings, it depended ultimately on the possession of force wherewith to drive men to His Will, as if God were a despot. That brings us to the very root of all our trouble. Our ideas of perfection are wrong. They are not the ideas that God has revealed to us, but our own. We do not reverence or worship the Right things or the Right people. We exalt the mighty to their seats, and put down the humble and meek. We still believe in and worship Force, and despise Love. We are willing to respect LOVE PROVIDED IT HAS FORCE BEHIND IT, but without that it seems to us still to be contemptible. Pure Love is still despised and rejected of men. It saves others and cannot save itself, and that to us is pure weakness. We are still ashamed of the Cross, and cannot stand the reckless humility of God. We are still cowards and snobs and sycophants at heart, and our real reverence and respect is still for physical force, wealth, luxury, and outward show. Even when we profess to despise these things we are not sincere. It is a case of the Fox and the Grapes, we pretend to despise what we cannot get. There is all the bitterness of thwarted desire in the contempt which the 'have nots' display for the 'haves.' Give them the chance, and they would change places to-morrow and be as blatantly vulgar and as stupidly tyrannical as those who in possession are to-day. The champions of the 'Bottom Dog' are only out to make him 'Top Dog,' not to make him a New Man. Those in possession taunt the dispossessed with envy, and their taunt is true, but they are too stupid and too blind to perceive that two wrongs can never make one right; and so we go round in the putrid circle of our own moral perversity, plunging the world into sorrow, and piercing our souls with pain, because we crucify the Son of God afresh, despising Love and not believing in its power. This problem of power is the very heart of our trouble. We have not grasped God's Truth revealed in Christ, because our idea of power is essentially wrong.

Our idea of power is not God's idea of power revealed in Christ, and it is not God's idea, because our purpose is not God's purpose, our will is not God's Will. Our idea of power depends upon our idea of purpose. It must. Whether a thing is powerful or not depends upon the purpose that you use it for. A bull is a powerful animal for the purpose of ploughing a field, but for the purpose of preserving delicate antiques in a china shop it is not powerful at all. The gentle hands of some frail woman would be power for that purpose. A locomotive engine is powerful for purpose of transport, but not for the purpose of teaching a child its alphabet. Our idea of God's Power depends upon our idea of God's purpose, and we cannot have a clear conception of His Power until we perceive with heart and mind that the purpose of God is Brotherhood, the Creation of 'Man,' the making of a united family of human beings.

When we have really got that perception clear and clean in our hearts and minds, then we begin to see that for God's purpose, which is the Creation of Man, the human family or unity, there is, and can be, only one Power, and that is Love. For that purpose force is not power, it is weakness. A unity of human beings is an imperfect unity just so far as it is based upon force and fear. That is the lesson that the history of these last strange years should have blasted into our minds. How much we hoped from the unity of the classes and nations in time of war, and how bitterly our hopes have been disappointed! It was a weak and superficial unity, because it was not based upon Love.

Again and again during the year after the war I listened to impassioned appeals to men to unite in the cause of Righteousness, appeals based upon the unity that we had attained and preserved during the war. 'Look what you have done,' cried the orators, 'look what you have done. Look how cliques and classes ceased to be, and a nation came to birth, fired with one spirit, buoyed with one hope, pressing onward like one man, on through the Valley of Death and the sorrows of Hell, on through seas of blood to ford triumphant Peace and final Victory. Look what you have done, why can you not do it again? Why need there be dissensions now and bitterness, why need we lose the splendid unity that was born mid the groans of our dead comrades on a thousand stricken fields?' Well, why need we? Simply because it was not a splendid, but an entirely superficial, unity, because it was not a unity of persons, it was a unity of bodies. A soldier in time of war is not a person but a puppet, who moves when you pull strings. The Army says to a man, 'Go - Go - or I'll shoot you,' and naturally a man goes under those circumstances. He is deprived of the freedom - the separate and spontaneous life - which is the essence of personality. That is why soldiers are often impatient with politicians. 'Why all this talk?' says the soldier, the simple, strong, and silent soldier. 'Why all this talk? Why don't you get the thing done?' Because, O silent, strong, and extremely simple (not to say fat-headed) soldier, my purpose is not your purpose, and my power is not your power. Your purpose is destruction, and mine is creation. Your power is compulsion, and mine is persuasion. Your very existence is the result of my weakness. You only come in where I fail. For creative purposes force is not strength, but the result of weakness, and it never creates anything. That is the very essence of the Christian Truth, and it is because we have failed to grasp it that we crave for a God with what we call 'absolute power,' Who is Master in His own universe, and are too blind to see that the foolishness of God is wiser than men, and the weakness of God is stronger than men, and why God hath chosen the foolish things of the world to confound the wise, and the weak things of the world to confound the things that are mighty. In the eyes of men there is no fool like God, because in the eyes of God there are no fools like men.

That does not mean that we should abolish all armaments and force to-morrow. It merely means that we should start out on the right basis and recognise that our armaments are symbols, not of our power, but of our weakness, that the great powers are the great weaknesses of our world. It means that we should recognise that we cannot attain to greatness by painting the map of the world red, but only by washing the soul of the world white. Our military power is an exact index of our spiritual and moral impotence.

Until we do recognise that, there can be no peace and no true progress. And so it is that when our minds are cleared of all confusion about the meaning of power, we begin to appreciate the truth of this first clause of our great Creed. There is a Spirit of Unity who works out His purpose throughout the process, and for that purpose - the Creation of Man, the Human Unity - there is no other Power but His, which is the Power of Love. God is Love, and all power belongs to Love.

There is more real power in that simple truth than there is in the massed armies and navies of all the nations of the world. There is more wealth in it than earth's million banks contain. There is more beauty in it than all the millionaires could buy. There is sufficient dynamite in it to blow our rotten civilisation sky high, and bring down the New Jerusalem out of Heaven, adorned as a bride for her husband. It is the only thing which can make our politics truly progressive and redeem our House of Commons from its exceeding commonness, which can heal the hurts of the suffering peoples and lift the everlasting burden from their souls. O God for a statesman who would stop quoting the Bible in the spirit of cheap and vulgar parody, or to deck the insincere peroration of a frothy clever speech, and would speak to the peoples with clear insight and vision begotten of this its crowning Truth!

Our supremest need is real faith in the omnipotence of Love. Thousands talk of God Almighty, and have no faith in Love at all; to them the real powers are force, wealth, competition, and self-interest. These are the powers that sway the world. They only believe that God made Heaven and Earth because if He didn't, then they don't know who the devil did. God to them is just the conventional name for The Great Unknown, about whom nothing is or can be certain. Orthodox infidels, they say their Creed and never base an action upon it, because they don't believe in Love. If you told them that God was not Almighty in the strict despotic sense, but that He had to strive and travail to bring His purpose to its birth, they would tell you that they could not accept such a degraded God as that. But this orthodox infidelity has no power to save the world. God is Love, the Spirit of Unity, Brotherhood, Co-operation,

Peace, and when we say our Creed we pledge ourselves to live, to think, act, and speak upon our faith in that spirit and in its power. It is impossible to prove that Love is almighty now; it does not reveal itself as supreme, but as struggling, striving, and conquering, calling us to fling ourselves in faith upon it, and prove it almighty in our lives. That is the sense of the Creed. It does not pledge you to the incredible belief that all this weird and awful process is the Will of an Almighty Despot; it pledges you to consecrate your whole life to the service of Love, that you may prove your faith in its final omnipotence in the only way it can be proved, by experience. When you realise this, the Creed rings out a question and a challenge: Do you believe in the power of Love? It is not a thing you can accept and let it make no difference to your life. It is no mere declaration that you accept the universe as it is, and believe vaguely that all is for the best. You do not hide behind a picturesque and pious agnosticism disguised as Reverence, and talk with bated breath about the awful mystery of omnipotence, and the folly of supposing that poor finite man can do anything but just submit to His inscrutable Providence.

You do not take refuge in that pride which apes humility, and insist upon calling God by splendid names that have no meaning. You do not plead that God is Eternal and you are temporal, and cannot do anything but accept the mystery. You declare your faith in the foolishness of the Gospel truth that the Eternal reveals itself through the temporal as Love, and that you propose to consecrate your every thought and word and deed to the service of that Love.

Said in that true sense, the Creed can save the World.

'Upward and onward I lead, lead on,
But my children are stupid and blind;
They start at shadows and turn them back,
Back to the mist and the mire behind,
To mists of falsehood and mire of lust,
Where cruelty lurks with gleaming eyes,
To spring at the soul of the world I win,
And glut on its blood till beauty dies.
Ever and ever I heal their wounds,
Pouring in life with my Blood Divine,
Soothing their sorrows and trembling fears,
Staying their hunger with Bread and Wine.
Every wound in the world I feel,
Every pang is a pang to me.
Deeper and deeper the nails strike through,
Count ye the cost of my Calvary.
Why should I suffer? - ye ask me - why?
Why not shatter the world into bits
And build it again a perfect whole
Where every part in the great plan fits?

36

'Have I no power to work my will?
Am I so weak that a mortal man
Can spit in my face, defy my word,
Can wrack and ruin my perfect plan?
What know ye about weakness and power?
Ye reckon of nought but force-brute force
Ye think of the world as a vast machine
And measure strength by strength of a horse.
Ye think it is power to blast and break
Masses of matter to powdered sand,
Ye think of destruction, murder, war,
Ye think of a bull or a giant's hand,
And then ye think of your God and ask,
Why is He suffering, helpless, weak?
Why does He plead when He ought to drive?
Why is His majesty all so meek?
Have I the power? All power is mine,
Yet am I weaker than yon small child.
I am the King of a million worlds,
I who am lowly in heart and mild.
Yet shall I conquer and win my way,
Casting the mighty men from their seat,
Lifting the humble to heights of power,
Trampling the haughty beneath my feet.
I am so weak that I bear a cross,
I am so strong that I need no crown,
I am the first and the last - Pure Love,
I lift the weight of the worlds alone.

'Your power is nought but an ancient fear,
Gripping your soul from the jungle home
Where your first parents with haunted eyes
At sunset left their lairs to roam
And seek for their prey by stealth, in fear
Lest a stronger beast than they should leap,
Swift death, to tear them with curved claws
And leave their babes to a hungry sleep.
Your power is weakness of fear like theirs,
Ye pile up terrors with trembling hands;
Behind your bulwarks of boasted power
The phantom of fear and darkness stands.
Because it is dark and my great light
Is but a glimmer to your blind eyes,
Ye put your trust in an idol God,
And crouch in his temple of lust and lies.

37

If all the might of the nations leagued
    Were massed in a host prepared to fight,
They would be as weak as a broken reed,
    Compared with a single shaft of light.
Your swords of steel and your iron ships
    Are shams that keep you in darkness still,
But Light and Love and Truth are powers
    That work and weave the eternal Will.

'Your kings and thrones and glittering crowns,
    Your shining sceptres and chains of gold,
Proclaim you children that play with toys,
    Poor damaged toys that are growing old,
Cutting your fingers with your toy knives,
    Breaking your hearts in your childish play,
Weeping hot tears for your broken dreams,
    Blind to the dawn of the coming day.
But power is mine, and is mine to give,
    Ever I give it with my heart's blood,
Nothing can stay it - the power of Love
    Lift up your eyes, and behold your God.
The night is passing, the hills grow grey,
    Awake I and hark to the watchman's cry
Love comes - I come; and the eastern way
    Splits into splendour as God draws nigh.'

IV.   *And in Jesus*

NOW where are we? Well, we have tried to look this rum world in the face, and in the light of what we know to discern what lies behind it. It is a weird face. It is a face as ugly as sin and as beautiful as an angel, as cruel as the sea and as tender as a woman. It is a world of stars and snakes, of violets and vermin, of laughter and tears, of peace and pain, of joy and sorrow, a world of contradiction. We determined that the great secret was to grasp the fact that it was a changing world, as changing as a face, with a change so slow as to be invisible, and so sure that no one could fail to see its results in time. It is not a finished creation, but an uncompleted growth. As such it must be judged in the light of its latest results like any other growth or movement. Nature must be judged in the light of human nature, and the best human nature - the martyrs, poets, saints, and saviours of the human race. Looked at like that, we cannot regard it as the result of an accident or an infinite series of accidents. It is like a difficult manuscript written in a language which we only understand in part; much of it looks like nonsense, but here and there a splendid sentence flashes out a glorious truth that goes straight to the inmost core of our understanding. It may be the life of a saint, or the works of a poet, but because of it we cannot regard the manuscript as the scribbling of an idiot, or as the trail of dirt left behind it by some mindless living thing; because of these great luminous sentences we must believe that the writing has an intelligence behind it. There must be something behind as great and greater than that which has come out of it. Life has come out of it, and therefore life must be behind it. Intelligence has come out of it, and therefore intelligence must be behind it. Personality has come out of it, and therefore there must be personality behind it. A unity of persons, a brotherhood, a family of persons seems to be coming out of it, therefore there must be a unity of persons behind it. I do not see how we are to get away from those conclusions even if we wanted to. Of course we can discuss them to no end, and chase a million red herrings dragged across the scent, but when we have indulged in mental gymnastics until the very tissue of our brains is bored, we come back to this. We must either refuse to take any stand at all, and decide to 'Wait and see,' - an attitude which is as ruinous in all living issues as it is in politics - either we must treat the universe as Mr. Asquith treated Ireland, with the same disastrous results, or we must believe in God the Father, Maker of Heaven and Earth. And if we are to live in the fullest sense, we must take the one step further, and add 'Almighty,' thus throwing ourselves body, mind, and spirit into the great task, believing that the Power which began will make an end, that the poem of life at last shall be complete, expressing perfect beauty. That must be our final faith

G A Studdert Kennedy

- 'I believe in God the Father Almighty, Maker of Heaven and Earth.' And it is strengthened because of the next step - because of Jesus. The Creed selects one flaming sentence out of Life's queer manuscript - the Life of Jesus. What are you going to make of this? it says. I know there are some queer and cruel sentences in the Book of Life. I know that many of its pages stink of blood and reek with corruption, but look at this sentence; did you ever read such perfect poetry, or listen to such splendid music, as this sentence that begins in the Manger and ends on the Cross contrives to express? Can we believe that a poem which contains lines like these is anything but the work of a consummate genius? Yes, I know it is very fragmentary, very sketchy. It is not a biography in our modern senses. There is no one consistent story in the Gospels. Mr. Arthur Drews and the German critics are right there. The Gospels are indeed a collection of fragmentary incidents. There is no one consistent story. But there is One consistent Character which grows out of these pages until the student sees a Face and hears a Voice. It is so consistent that a thousand men can meet together and talk of Him, knowing that they have a common Friend, discovering again and again with a thrill that down widely different paths, and in all sorts of peculiar ways, the same Person has come to each of them out of the Gospel page. The critic may come in with his spectacles, scissors, and paste; he may take the Gospels to pieces and put them together again, but when he has finished the Voice still speaks, and the Eyes of Jesus still ask questions of the soul. The Character still stands, and calmly makes its challenge: Which of you convinceth Me of sin? In every age the challenge has been taken up, and men have railed on Jesus ever since He died. They have declared again and again that He was out of date, that He was dead and ought to be buried. Some have attacked Him scornfully, with bitter anger in their eyes; some have forsaken Him sadly, with lingering regrets. But somehow He always appears to be the final judge of His judges. Nietzsche spurns His humility and dubs Him a slave, and then dies in a madhouse, and becomes a byword in Europe as the author of a gospel that leads the world to Hell. The pioneers of progress proclaim Him a reactionary, and then find themselves at a dead end with their reforms, because they need a 'New Spirit' among the peoples; and it grows more evident every day that the New Spirit which they seek is as old as Jesus and as new. The critics contradict themselves, and cut one another out. Some say He is too joyful, some say He is too sad. Some say He is too gentle, and some that He is too hard. To some He pipes and they will not dance, to others He mourns and they will not weep. But it all ends in this. With silent insistence the Character criticises the critics. If a man or woman or an age of men and women reject the Character, they do it at their peril, and time makes the peril plain. An age of luxury may reject His discipline, but time makes it clear that they are wrong. An age of materialism may reject His idealism, but their children will come seeking it again. An age of

40

Puritanism may condemn His gaiety and gentleness, but the pendulum will swing back again. An age of scientific knowledge may spurn His simplicity, but men come back with out-stretched arms and empty hearts to ask the real questions that learning leaves unanswered for the soul. If a man or a woman rejects the Character, I find myself wondering what is the matter with them, where is the yellow streak? They may reject organised Christianity and be white men; they may reject it because it is not like Jesus. They may reject orthodox theology because it puts their mind into a muddle, and does not seem worthy of Jesus. They may reject the 'Divinity of Christ' because the words have come to mean something incredible and absurd to them. They may reject Jesus as God, but if they turn from Him as Man, Man with a capital M, Man as He ought to be, then I wonder about them - what's wrong? With a mercifully merciless finger Jesus points to the weak spot in every character and in every age. A learned critic explains Him away, lays bare the inconsistencies and improbabilities of the Gospel stories; and just as one rises convinced, one sees the Finger pointing to pride - pride of intellect, the old idolatry of the mind - and one sees that the whole argument is based upon assumptions, and depends for its force upon an atmosphere. It belongs to the study, and not to the street; culture cannot take the place of Christ, the Character still stands. An ardent Socialist curses Jesus as an enemy of progress, a milk-and-water Saviour, and one is impressed; and then the Finger points to envy, hatred, malice, and the bitterness of disappointed ambition, and the pages of rhetoric lose their force, because one sees the man. A man of the world mocks at Him, and in the atmosphere of the smoke-room He seems absurd; and then the Finger points at the man's mouth, the scales fall from one's eyes, and one sees in the faces of these cultivated gentlemen naked animalism, and the sordid dreariness of the brothel comes into it all - one feels as if there were a bad smell. I sit after dinner with a man who argues cleverly on grounds of humanity that His ideas of purity were ridiculously severe. He seems so broad-minded and so kind that one is nearly convinced; and then it all comes out the poor devil is in a moral mess, wandering round and round in the eternal triangle where there is no argument but one. Again and again it happens, and most of all in one's self. I want to reject Him, get rid of Him, and be free. I invent a thousand reasonable excuses and objections - circumstances alter cases; He belonged to another age - but the Finger goes on pointing to the spot, and in my heart I know it is true. In a world of wild uncertainties, new discoveries, and new theories the Character still stands and judges them right or wrong.

The wonder of the Gospel is not the one consistent story, but the One consistent Character that shines out through all the stories. And so, when a learned critic dismisses Jesus as the literary invention of Mark, 'a figure swimming obscurely in the midst of tradition,' one cannot help feeling that it is the conclusion of a man whose mind is almost as mixed as his own metaphors, a man whose life has been lived second-hand, lived among books and not among people. There is no good entering into an argument with a mind like that upon this question; it would end nowhere, because it would be all on the wrong plane. It would be like arguing with a botanist on the beauty of Browning, or discussing Rakmananoff's Prelude with a professional piano-tuner. Scientific method has its limitations, and it simply is not applicable to questions involving this kind of moral issue. If John Mark invented Jesus, then there existed at that time a literary genius before whom Shakespeare pales into utter insignificance. That this Character should be pure invention involves to my mind a greater miracle than the Resurrection. I cannot believe it. Purely on His own Authority - the Authority of His moral Beauty - Jesus stands across the ages as Man - Perfect Man. But was He more than Man? He was human. was He Divine? When you ask that you open the floodgates to an interminable river of talk, if you get down on to the intellectual plain. To the making of books in attack and defence of the Divinity of Jesus Christ there is no end, and the study of them is not merely a weariness to the flesh, it is a positive poison to the spirit; they obscure the real issue. Thousands of good men who would admit that He was Perfect Man, that His was the Perfect Life, resent the doctrine of His Divinity, simply because it seems to make Him inhuman, to remove Him from the practical into the visionary, out of the natural into the supernatural. They want a man, and not a miracle. They want a natural human Jesus, not a supernatural Christ. Mr. Edward Carpenter, in his book on *Pagan and Christian Creeds,* comes out with this judgment: 'Personally I must say I think the "legendary" solution quite likely, and in some ways more satisfactory than the opposite one, for the simple reason that it seems more encouraging to suppose that the story of Jesus (gracious and beautiful as it is) [Good old fellow, out comes the Character claiming its own - that's me, not Mr. Carpenter; he would start to qualify it, because it is beneath his intellectual dignity to be a Christian] is a myth which gradually formed itself in the conscience of mankind, and thus points the way of humanity's future evolution, than to suppose it to be the mere record of a unique and miraculous interposition of Providence which depends entirely upon the Powers above, and could hardly be expected to occur again.'

If I have to choose between these two notions, I would agree with Mr. Carpenter; but I don't see why I should choose. I don't think either of them is true. I don't think the Life of Jesus is a myth. That theory is far-fetched-fetched out of brains that feed on books, not out of experience that feeds on life. I don't think the Life of Jesus was 'a unique and miraculous interposition of Providence which depends entirely upon the Powers above.' I don't understand what that means. It seems to separate the Life of Jesus from the rest of life, it seems to separate the rest of life from the Powers above. It divides the natural and the supernatural into two water-tight compartments. That is what I think is all wrong. Humanity and Divinity - God and man - are not two mutually exclusive ideas, they are not like oil and water that won't mix. Dear Lord, how much muddle there has been over that notion. Jesus was supposed to be God and man - two separate things combined into a supernatural unity, but never mingled. At one time He acted and spoke as God, and at another as man; and the result was, you never knew where you had Him, and He appeared aloof and impossible. 'Of course he was God, and we cannot be like Him.' That was the idea, and it destroys the whole essence of Christianity. I cannot separate Jesus from the process. He was and is its Crown. He was one with all life as I am. He was one with earth and sky and sea, with birds and beasts and fishes, aye, and one with pterodactyls and dinosauri, and protoplasmic unicellular amœbæ, and all the rest of the queer creatures with barbarous scientific names that play a part in the ascent of man. He was one with all life. He summed up the meaning of it all, and so revealed the Creator of it all. He issued out of the process because He had been in it from the beginning, or rather it had been in Him; through Him all things were made, and without Him was not anything made which was made. He is the Head of the human race, and the human race is the Head of nature. You must judge nature in the light of human nature, and you must judge human nature in the light of Jesus, and so you must judge the whole process in the light of Jesus. It meant Jesus from the beginning. All that we can know about the Author of the Process is to be found in Him. He is to us God, because He is Perfect Man. He is God speaking to us in the only language we can understand, which is the human language, God revealed to us in the only form that we have eyes to see, which is the human form. He was as natural as a jelly-fish and as supernatural as the New Jerusalem coming down from heaven, adorned as a bride for her husband.

If there was a unique and miraculous interposition of Providence, it was as unique and as miraculous as the interposition which took place when organic issued out of inorganic matter, or when mind issued out of matter. His Life marked a stage in the drama of development. He was as natural and as supernatural as a cabbage, and His Life 'depended as entirely upon the Powers above' as the life of a cauliflower does. You think it is irreverent to say that Jesus was as natural as a cabbage or cauliflower. That is because you have never seen a cabbage. You have never stopped and stared at one as though it were the first cabbage in the world. You have fallen into the ridiculous error of supposing that, whereas the first vegetable was a wondrous mystery that no mind can ever fathom, the billion-billionth vegetable is a perfectly simple thing that a fool can understand, which is an idea almost idiotic in its simplicity. Every cabbage is more wonderful than the last, and adds more mystery to the first, because the mystery of preservation is added to the mystery of creation. It is not I that am irreverent, it is you. It is not that I do not see God in Jesus, it is you that do not see Him in cabbages. You would in lilies, of course, because Jesus happened to mention lilies as revelations of God, and besides, they are nicer looking. 'Behold the lilies of the field' sounds quite reverent and dignified, but 'Behold the cabbage in the allotment patch' well, that is making fun. But what tomfoolery that is. Cabbages are just as divine as lilies; both mean Jesus, Who is the Crown of Life, the Image of the Father. That is the truth of the Incarnation. It explains all life in terms of Jesus Christ. Jesus was as unique and miraculous as the first man. There never could be another first man, and there never could be another Jesus. Both were unique and miraculous revelations of God, but, of course, Jesus was the higher revelation. The first Adam was made a living soul, the second Adam was a quickening, a life-giving Spirit. Every fresh Christian - every soul that is born again and finds in Him the New Man, the New Life, and the Peace of God, adds to the wonder of Jesus, and makes Him more unique; and we shall never know all that Jesus was until we all come to the measure of the stature of the fullness of Christ. It is not necessary to suppose that Jesus was a myth that gradually formed itself in the conscience of mankind, in order that He may point the way of humanity's future evolution. He does that because He was a reality, and can only do it with any certainty if He was a reality.

In Jesus Man with a capital M, Man the Human Unity or Brotherhood, was born. He was the Incarnate Brotherhood of Man revealing the Eternal Fatherhood of God. He was Humanity Incarnate. How true that is to practical life! Was He not the Incarnation of all that we mean by 'Humanity'? That was the Truth behind the title that above all others Jesus loved to claim - Son of Man. It was, of course, a title that He took from the common parlance of the day in order to give it a new meaning, to interpret it in His own way - a way which profoundly shocked and scandalised the religious people of His day. They thought of the Son of Man as a despot; Jesus said He was a servant. They thought He was a conqueror; Jesus said He was a sufferer. They thought He had come to reign; Jesus said He had come to die. It was as Son of Man that He forgave sins, it was as Son of Man that He came to seek and to save that which was lost, it was as Son of Man that He was betrayed into the hands of wicked men, was mocked and spit on, crucified and rose again. It is as Son of Man He claims to judge the world. He was the very spirit of perfect humanity, and that was His title to Divinity. Because, of course, man's God must be Perfect Man. What other God could we know or love? He never acted as God and not man. He never acted as man and not God. All His actions, all His thoughts, words, and deeds were human thoughts, words, and deeds revealing God. He was all that we can ever know of God, because 'He was all that we can ever know of man.

It is because we have not grasped this truth, because we have clung to the letter of the metaphors in which He strove to express His Being and

His Mission, because we have insisted on a supernatural Christ in a way that raised up in men's minds the picture of an unnatural Jesus, that you get men - good men and white - telling you that while they love Jesus as the best man that ever lived, they cannot believe in His Divinity or in God at all. Humanity is their god, they will tell you. Humanity is what they believe in and live for; it is the tragic drama of the martyrdom of man that has gripped hold of them and called them; humanity that Christians tell them was left for ages in a fallen state, and then given a chance of salvation - a chance that only seems to have been taken by a tiny fraction of all the countless millions that have sinned and suffered, laughed, loved, lived, and died beneath the sun. It is the race they love and live for. This is the inspiration of the Socialist, so far as he is a real Socialist, and not a common or garden thief. This is the inspiration of the doctor, the scientist, the educationalist, and of all that mighty host of men and women who have gone out to conquer, refusing the Sign of the Cross because it stood to them not for the martyrdom of God in man, but merely for the martyrdom of man by God, or Fate, or the Great Unknown. This is the inspiration of a million men whom Jesus would have looked upon and loved, saying wistfully, 'Thou art not far from the Kingdom of God.' 'Not everyone that saith unto Me, Lord, Lord,' not every one that accepts the dogma of My Divinity, 'shall enter into the Kingdom of Heaven, but He that doeth the Will of My Father which is in Heaven.' It is this great host that Jesus longs to claim - not that He is jealous that they should bear His name, but because He has a power to give them that they have not got, a peace to bestow upon them which they do not know. These are the men and women that must be brought within the fold of the Catholic Church, if that Church is to save the world. What keeps them out? Often just the noblest that is within them; their sense of justice, mercy, pity bids them side with man the martyr against the God who martyrs man. A false conception of God. What they need is just what they could find in God revealed in Jesus, God in Man; it would add to their Love, Faith and Hope. Love they have, but it is often faithless and hopeless, based upon despair. They cannot believe in humanity as it is now, they cannot worship this chaos of conflicting passions and sordid self-interests, this weltering mass of discordant individuals that make the world of men; they need humanity as it is in Jesus, humanity caught up into God, to transform and uplift their Loving Service and fill it with the fire of Faith. They must worship the Spirit of humanity, which is crucified and tortured in the world of men, and it is that very Spirit which reveals its perfection in Jesus, and in Him can draw near, nearer than breathing, nearer than hands and feet. They have the Christian ethic, they need the Christian religion. It is only as religion that humanitarianism can become a vital force transforming character and making men anew. And that is the great need of all humanitarians to-day. They have already a passion to give what they have: they give time, money, intelligence, labour, but the one thing they have not is spiritual force, redemptive power. That is why all their schemes are futile and barren. Human nature bars the way, bars the way to lasting peace between the nations, to real co-operation between the classes, real unison between the sexes, bars the way to the Creation of Man. The honest Socialist breaks his heart because men are not social, the noble reformer frets and fumes because men will not be reformed, the keen politician despairs of politics because they are so sordid and so mean, the earnest Christian sorrows because men will not come to Christ. Part of that burden they all must bear because human nature is imperfect and sinful, but part of it can be removed if the barricade of false conceptions and old outworn ideas could be broken down, and men be called to the Great Adventure, called to make their great bet on God revealed in Jesus, God suffering in Man. If all the honest but limited lovers of man could be united with all the honest but limited lovers of God, an army might be formed which, under the Sign of the Cross, might go forth to save the world, because it would have in it, not only Love, but Faith and Hope as well, and in these three the power it needs, not merely to save men from their sorrow but to save them from their sin.

V.   *Christ*

THE challenge of the Christian Creed thus far amounts to this. Life is a gallant gamble, and you must either bet or cease to live, and be content to linger. Will you bet your heart-strings on the Author of the weird and wondrous process by which the world and men have come to be, believing that He has a purpose, which is the Creation of Man, the Human Unity, Brotherhood, Family, believing in Him as God the Father, Maker of Heaven and Earth, Who has within Him power to carry His purpose out to its appointed end? Will you go further and bet that His character is displayed to us in Jesus of Nazareth, Who was the Perfect Man, and is therefore the Revelation of man's God? Then it goes on and adds to that name which it puts above all other names a title. It adds to the name of Jesus the title 'Christ.' Well, what does that mean? Does it extend the challenge further, or is it an empty title of honour? What does the Creed mean by asking us to believe in Jesus as the Christ? It is a title with a long and romantic history. Round it, for those who know its story, there gathers a surging multitude of human hopes, aspirations, and desires, which have found utterance in a mass of legends, myths, religious rites, and ceremonies in every age and in every corner of the world. 'Christos' is the Greek translation of the Hebrew 'Messiah' which means the 'Anointed One,' and was the title of the great Deliverer, Saviour, or Redeemer whom the Jews believed would come to save the world from sorrow and from sin. But this expectation, this passionate longing for a Saviour, was not confined to the Jewish race, it was literally world wide. To quote Mr. Edward Carpenter's book on *Pagan and Christian Creeds, their Origin and Meaning:* 'The number of Pagan Deities (mostly virgin born and done to death in some way or other in their efforts to save mankind) is so great as to be difficult to keep account of. The God Krishna in India, the God Indra in Nepaul and Thibet, spilt their blood for the salvation of mankind. Buddha said, according to Max M&uum;ller, "Let all the sins that were in the world fall on me, that the world may be delivered." The Chinese Tien, the Holy One, "one with God, and existing with Him from all eternity," died to save the world. The Egyptian Osiris was called Saviour; so was Horus; so was the Persian Mithras; so was the Greek Hercules, who overcame death, though his body was consumed in the burning garment of mortality, out of which he rose to Heaven. So also was the Phrygian Attis called Saviour, and the Syrian Tammuz or Adonis likewise, both of whom were nailed or tied to a tree, and afterwards rose again from their biers or coffins. Prometheus, the greatest and earliest benefactor of the human race, was nailed by the hands and feet with arms extended to the rocks of Mount Caucasus. Bacchus or Dionysius, born of the Virgin Semele to be the liberator of mankind (Dionysius Eleutherios as he was called), was torn to pieces, not unlike Osiris. Even in far-off Mexico, Quetzalcoatl, the Saviour, was born of a Virgin, was tempted, and fasted forty days, and was done to death.'

Now, when you come to think of it, that is a queer business, isn't it? Here you have peoples so utterly severed and disconnected that there is no possibility of communication between them, and yet there grows up among them spontaneously, as it were, a passionate longing for a Saviour - a Deliverer - a Christ. 'The long tradition of the Saviour comes down from the remotest times, and perhaps from every country in the world.' Funnily enough, this has often been used as an argument against the reality of the 'Christ.' The fact that the Messianic passion was not confined, as most of us were taught in the days of our youth, to the Jews, but was almost as universal among men of every race as hunger or thirst, is supposed to make it harder to believe that a 'Christ or Saviour' has ever come, or ever will. When it is discovered that all the world over men were holding up helpless hands to Heaven in supplication for a Saviour, and that the Old Testament only records one part of the age-long preparation for His coming, we are told that this conclusively proves that He never came. Learned men trace the history of this passion back through all the maze of legends, myths, rites and ceremonies that make up the history of man's search for God; they discover that it had immoral or non-moral beginnings, that it was connected with Nature Worship and the Sex Instinct, and then tell us that, having explained its origin, they have not only explained the passion, but have actually explained it away, and proved it to be a delusion. But that is a queer way of doing things. It is the topsy-turvy method of argument that the idolatry of the scientific method has imposed upon the world of men for years.

The analysis of a thing is supposed to be a complete account of it. Find out where a thing came from, and you know what it is. Prove that a man is grown from an egg, and you have explained the man. Of course it is all nonsense. It is not the beginning of a thing that explains its end, it is the end that explains the beginning. You cannot explain a passion or a plant by discovering where it comes from, you can only explain by discovering what it is coming to. If all the world over, a passionate desire for a saviour and deliverer sprang up, if black and white, red and yellow men have felt the passion burning in their hearts, so that they have burst into poetry, invented legends, and instituted rites and ceremonies to express it, the only thing that would really explain such a mysterious fact is not the discovery of the long process of its growth from strange beginnings - that only deepens the mystery - but the discovery of some great reality towards which it was leading men. Of course, if you believe that all the worlds were made by chance, or accident, there is no use asking for an explanation of that, or of anything else; it is all muddle, and there is no good thinking at all. But if you refuse to take up that attitude, the logical result of which is mental and moral suicide, if you take up the challenge of the Creed thus far, believing that a purpose runs through the ages of creative movement, then this circle of saviours that rings the whole world round would seem to point onwards to some one, or something, some great reality that would explain it. The real object of studying the history of this Messianic passion is not so much to discover where it came from, as to find out from its history what it is tending to.

If you study it in that way, some big broad facts grow clear. The passion, like most other human passions, as it develops seems to undergo a process of refinement. It seems to grow from the passionate longing for a magical and material salvation into the longing for a moral and spiritual one. Men seem at first to long for a Saviour who will do something for them, and later for a Saviour who will do something in them. First, they desire a Deliverer who will change their circumstances and surroundings, and then a Deliverer who will change them. Of course, it seems absurd to summarise so shortly a process which took ages, but, broadly speaking, that seems true. First, men seem to find the root of all their sorrows in the world without them, and later become conscious that the trouble really rises from the world within. These two strains in the passion do not, of course, succeed one another in an orderly sequence, nothing ever develops that way. Wherever the passion is found these two strains are found in it, but in some races the one is the stronger, and in other races the other. And as men grow in intelligence and insight the moral and spiritual passion grows stronger, and the magical and material more weak. The reason why the history of the preparation for the coming of the Christ among the Jews has gripped the Western world and survived to be read and loved by common men, while the history of that preparation among other peoples has barely survived to be hunted up out of the dust of ages by scholars, is that the great Jewish teachers and prophets had a clearer vision of the truth that what men needed was a moral and spiritual redemption - a Saviour who would change the world within.

I do not mean to say that the Jews were the only ones to see that truth, or that there is not a great deal of the lower strain in their passion for a Saviour. Neither of these statements would be true. The popular idea of Salvation among the Jews was as material and as magical as most popular conceptions; and the best of their teachers were not free from its influence. On the other hand, some of the legends and sayings current among so-called 'Pagan' peoples show great moral beauty and an intense longing for spiritual Salvation. We have no right that I can see to say that all the other sacred books were purely human and the Old Testament alone Divine, that they were merely Folklore, while the Old Testament is Revelation. That creates a division between the human and the Divine which cannot really exist. But we have a right to say that in the Old Testament story of the preparation we do see the higher truth, the loftier idea of Salvation, struggling more successfully to expression. We have a right to say that in the battle of the sacred books for survival the Bible won a foremost place, mainly on its merits, because of its deeper moral and spiritual appeal, because it touched mom's consciences and made them long to be better men in a way that other sacred writings failed to do.

I do not think there is any doubt that we have grossly underrated the moral and spiritual worth of other religions, and have allowed prejudice to blind our eyes to their beauty, and to the foreshadowing of Christ which they contain. It is a tragedy that we should have allowed a spirit of almost savage exclusiveness to have blotted out for us the revelation of God contained in earth's million myths and legends, so that Christians have regarded them almost as though they were the inventions of the evil one. It is a disaster that we should have lumped all other faiths together and called them 'Pagan' - dismissing them as worthless. It is disastrous because it has distorted our missionary methods and delayed the development of the world religion. It has made us seek to convert the East not merely to Christ, but to our peculiarly Western Christ, and to force upon other peoples not merely our experience of Him, but our ways of expressing the experience. It is disastrous, too, because it has bred in us the spirit of intolerance and contempt for others which is one of the chiefest obstacles to the union of the world. Perhaps, like other evil things, intolerance was an inevitable accompaniment of development, but it is none the less evil. It has led us to stress and emphasise comparatively unimportant issues in our statement of belief, and to elevate our own peculiarities into the position of principles. It has led us to trust in hatred rather than in love. It has caused us to put prejudice before truth, and to make a virtue of our own stupidity and ignorance. It has often made us orthodox liars for the glory of God. It has thrown us back upon futile and unchristian methods of defending our faith and spreading it abroad, and turned us from the one method which has in it the secret of success, the method of living by it, of basing our every thought, word, and deed upon its truth. It has made us fearful and distrustful of the power of Christ to win, and bred in us a blasphemous anxiety to do God's work for Him, and to build up defences for His Church, with human hands and human minds, when it needs no defences but its own eternal truth. It has thus delayed the coming of the day, which must inevitably come, when the faith which has in it most of truth and perfect moral beauty will win the world to the unity of the Spirit in the bonds of lasting peace.

I do not think there can be any doubt that we have paid, and are paying, for this mistake, a heavy price both at home and abroad, and that one of our chiefest lessons to be learned is that bigotry is no adequate substitute for faith. But when we have admitted all that, the fact still remains that in the Old Testament story of the Messianic passion, and the preparation for the coming of the Christ, the real meaning of the passion comes out more clearly than in any other, and it is true that we can search the Scriptures for witness to the Christ.

But all this is ancient history you say - very ancient, and in fact a bit mouldy. What has it got to do with the issues of to-day? It may have been important for a Jew at the time of Jesus to see that He fulfilled the prophecies upon which his fathers lived, but what has it got to do with me in the year of grace 1920? What do I care whether the Jews were God's sole chosen people, or whether there was a great light breaking through all over the world? I am willing to admit that the latter seems a more rational and likely notion, but how does it affect my belief one way or other?

Well, you see, this Messianic passion and its growth are part of the history of the world; they are a section of the wonderful process by which man's mental and emotional world has been built up, and the study of that process is at least as important for purposes of truth as the study of the process by which the material world was built. And it has to be looked at and judged in the same way. The way to learn from the past is to remember always that the whole universe is a movement, and must be examined with a view to discovering what it is moving to - what its purpose is. We have seen that this Messianic passion is a developing, growing passion, which, as it grows, tends to change its content. It grows from being a desire for a magical and material Saviour to being a desire for a moral and spiritual one. It is a passion almost as universal as hunger and thirst; and unless the world is a joke, or a chance, it must have a meaning and a purpose. We can best judge of its purpose in the light of its latest development. In its latest development it is seen as a passion for inward and spiritual Salvation, the longing for a Saviour who will not merely change man's lot but will change his heart, redeem his character. If it points onward, as we are driven to believe, to some great reality which will be food for its hunger and drink for its thirst, we should expect that it would be a great moral and spiritual reality. We should expect that the great passion for redemption of the inner man would find satisfaction at last in the appearance upon the earth of a Perfect Character, possessing the power of drawing men upwards into its own likeness. We have seen that the wonder of the Gospel stories is that out of them, with all their inconsistencies, there grows a supremely consistent Character which does possess this power of drawing men upwards into its own likeness. This has been the universal Christian experience. 'We all, with unveiled face reflecting as in a mirror the glory of the Lord, are transformed into the same image, from glory unto glory, as from the Lord - the Spirit.' This has been the experience not merely of the great saints who have left their record behind them, and made their mark upon the shifting sands of time, but it has been the experience, the fundamental experience, of millions of unknown saints who, by gallant, lives of self-sacrifice and love, of purity and passionate charity, have bravely borne the burden of the worlds, and done their part unseen in our development as a race. The history of the Christian Church, like the life of its Lord, is a tragedy, and often a sordid and revolting tragedy, but through it all there runs a vein of golden goodness that redeems its squalor and its ugliness. A man who can write: 'With the exception of a few episodes like the formation during the Middle Ages of the noble brotherhoods and sisterhoods of friars and nuns, dedicated to the help and healing of suffering humanity, and the appearanceof a few real lovers of mankind (and the animals) like St. Francis (and these manifestations can hardly be claimed by the Church which pretty consistently opposed them), it may be said that after the fourth century the real spirit and life of early Christian enthusiasm died away,' as Mr. Edward Carpenter does, is looking at history as a journalist looks at life - from the sensationalist point of view. No saint is worth bothering about who does not make a name for himself, and the Church is to be judged by the faults and failings, the sordid sins and squabbles that mar the history of its highest officials. But the history of the Papacy is no more the history of the Church than the history of the British Cabinet is the history of the British People. That judgment is a vulgar judgment, vulgar with the pernicious vulgarity of intellectual pride which lives in the world of books, and lives in that world without the imagination that comes of touch with real human sorrow, and with real human sin. The fire of Christian enthusiasm has at times burned low, but it has never died; it remains the soul of Western civilisation and the hope of all the world. And it is because this Character of Jesus meets the Messianic passion of mankind at its purest and best, and can prove itself bread for its hunger and wine for its thirst, that we claim for Jesus the title of the Christ.

And this adds to the challenge of the Creed for to-day. The Messianic passion is not dead. It is very much alive. There is in the world of to-day a very intense conviction, which after the last five years ought to be more intense, that there is still something wrong - radically wrong. And there is, too, a longing which is intense and ought to be intenser for some one or something to put it right. The Messianic passion is still there, and the two strains in it are still evident. There are those who long for a magical and material redemption, for a saviour or a system which will change man's lot, and make the world an entirely pleasant and comfortable place to live in, and there are a smaller number who have seen deeper and know that man's great need is moral and spiritual redemption, a Saviour who will not merely change man's lot but transform man's soul, and who perceive that only so can man's lot be changed - by the changing of his heart.

To take up the challenge of the Creed and bet your life upon Jesus as 'Christ' means that you throw in your lot with this smaller number. To believe in Jesus as the Christ means that you stand irrevocably opposed to the million and one Godless and materialistic schemes of redemption in which the world abounds. It confronts you with the same choice exactly as that which faced Jesus of Nazareth. He came to a race in which the Messianic passion was intense, and found the people longing for a Saviour, but mostly longing for the lower kind of Saviour - a military

Messiah Who would lead a great revolt and set God's people free; a National Deliverer Who would conquer the Roman conquerors and drive them from the land, and then take His power and reign in justice, restoring the Kingdom of Peace and Prosperity to suffering Israel. Expectation was keen, thousands were ready to rise, only waiting for a leader and a signal. The Kingdom of God which John the Baptist proclaimed meant to many of his hearers an earthly kingdom of Peace and Plenty and National Freedom. They sought a Saviour Who would change the world without. There were a smaller number - very small - who looked for a higher kind of Saviour, a Deliverer Who would come to save not merely Israel from its sorrow, but the whole world from its sin. Very few indeed, if any, had this idea of the Messiah, pure and uncontaminated by any lower elements; probably even the best had an idea of an earthly kingdom, in which righteousness should rule, and which would be founded by a great supernatural Leader Who would compel His enemies to submit. None saw the Truth as Jesus saw it. None fully grasped the fact that those who take the sword must perish by it, and that the everlasting Kingdom must be built on Faith and not Force. Jesus had to choose between the higher interpretation of His Mission and the lower, between the material Salvation which the people craved and the spiritual Salvation which they really needed. He chose the higher path, and in that choice lies at once the triumph and the tragedy of His Life. Once that choice was made, Calvary, or something like it, was inevitable, and on that choice, and on the way in which He carried it into action, depends His claim to be The Christ, The Saviour of the world.

That choice still pierces to the heart of our most modern problems. Still bright within the soul of man the Messianic passion burns, and still the two strains in it persist. The world is full of movements, plans, and schemes to better the world without bettering the souls of men, to obtain material without moral and spiritual Salvation. There is still the bitterness caused by tyranny and oppression, the tyranny of force, vested interests, financial scheming and wire-pulling-the whole of the sordid forces of reaction which remain in the hands of those who find this world satisfactory and sufficient for their small souls as it is, and would not have it changed. This secret slimy selfishness that saps the life-blood of the nations and feeds on the sorrows of the poor and friendless is still there, piercing us through with many sorrows, plunging the world into wars, worming its way into our politics, breeding rot and corruption in high places. It is still there, doing the dirty work it has done for centuries. And it still causes the passion for deliverance to burn in men's souls. The ruling classes still stand over against the ruled, the governors against the governed. And, as in Christ's day, so in ours, many believe that Salvation can be won by violence and threats of violence, by meeting force with force, and tyranny with counter tyranny. The vision of the great proletarian republic, when the workers shall rule the world, is held before us as the ideal end. Salvation must come through class war and the victory of the down-trodden and oppressed. The modern zealots - Socialists, Syndicalists, Class-conscious Proletarians - still proclaim war on the hated bourgeoisie, bidding us believe that you have only to destroy the competitive system of industry, and the rule of the classes over the masses, and earth will be a paradise. Everywhere we are forming ourselves into great fighting unions to secure our own interests, and we are told that when the Union of the Unions comes, and the people rise as one man, then the day of salvation will dawn for men. That on the one side, and all the cynical forces of reaction on the other, and the common man of all classes blind and bewildered between the two, that is the world of to-day. And the only light in it is still Jesus, the Christ. The Character stands firm and judges these movements right or wrong, or disentangles the mixture of right and wrong which makes them so bewildering to the honest man of the day who has to earn his bread and keep his children. Jesus stands and tells us that force is folly and hatred waste of time, that 'a man's life consisteth not in the multitude of things that he possesseth,' that there is more in life than pleasure, that giving is better than gain, that the secret of life is service and self-sacrifice.

He is, of course, despised and rejected by both sides. The reactionaries patronise Him and render Him lip-service, but in their hearts believe that He is quite unpractical and does not count. The revolutionaries hate Him, and declare that His Gospel of Love is opium to the people, who need to be fed fat with hatred, that they may be strong to revolt. Business is business, and Christ has nothing to do with it, says the commercialist. 'Conscious labour or planned organisation of social labour is the name of the expected Messiah of the New Age. Our hope of Salvation is not a religious ideal, but rests on the massive foundation stone of materialism,' says Mr. Belfort Bax, the Socialist. Christ tells the business man that he is an immoral scoundrel, and the Socialist that he is a silly fool, and points another way. That is the glory of the Creed. You know where you are, your principles are fixed. Men can't come plucking you by the arm and saying, 'Lo here' and 'Lo there' - this theory, that theory; they cannot turn you after a New Messiah every week; you know that what is wanted is the transformation of the human heart into His likeness, and that all schemes are futile which are not aimed at that, and all plans wrong which are not based upon it. You know that the stone which the builders rejected is become the headstone of the corner, and that whatever scheme runs up against that stone must in time be broken to pieces. You know that these two parties make a lot of noise, beating their tom-toms and blowing their own trumpets, but that *the real revolution is a silent steady change* which takes place in the world as men, women, and children see the great light, and turn to the Character of Christ as their lodestar, and are inspired with His Spirit as their motive-power-as they realise that Jesus is Christ.

VI.   *His only Son?*

THE next note of the Christian challenge adds much to its meaning and more to its emphasis, and that is an important addition, for often Truth is distorted by over or under emphasis of its many sides. The Creed proceeds to underline in red ink the claim of Jesus to be the Perfect Revelation of the Character of God in terms of human personality and the Saviour of the world from sin. It piles it on, so to speak, and, not content with claiming for Him the title of the Christ, it adds, 'His only Son our Lord.' There is to be no mistake about it, because He is the power-centre of the whole challenge. The Nicene Creed bursts into poetry over it, and calls Jesus 'God of God, Light of Light, Very God of Very God, Begotten not made, being of one substance with the Father, by Whom all things were made.' It is impossible to attach literal and exact meanings to each of those glowing symbols. The whole thing is like a fanfare of trumpets or the roll of a thousand drums, emphasising the conviction that in Jesus God reveals Himself to man, lays bare His heart, and shows what He is like. There is, of course, a note of defiance in the emphasis, it is the challenge that replies to an attack. Jesus was a very good man, or a very beautiful myth, says the world, but, of course, it is childish to say that He was the image of God. No man could be that, the infinite cannot be completely revealed in the finite. You degrade the whole idea of God when you contend that He became man, and revealed Himself in Jesus of Nazareth. Jesus may have been a great prophet and seer who proclaimed High Truths about God, but to say that He was His Image, 'His only Son,' as you put it, that He is to be worshipped and recognised as absolute Lord of men's lives - well, we do not want to be nasty, because we respect your opinions, but it is nonsense, you know. Be a bit reasonable, and draw it mild, and we are willing to go with you. We are quite willing to give Jesus a high place - perhaps the highest - in the gallery of the world's good men. We are willing to admit that He was the greatest religious genius that has ever appeared on earth. We are willing to give great weight to His teaching when it is practical and reasonable, but, of course, you know a great deal of it is too good for this world, and He was rather a dreamer, wasn't He? It wouldn't work in business, would it? What? Consider the lilies, and the ravens - very nice idea - but, well - business is business, and men are not angels. Besides, this idea of the Fall, and then the ages of preparation, and then God sending down His Son to die - after a miraculous birth - it is beautiful and romantic, but it cannot be literal truth, can it? It involves so many queer antiquated ideas. Now, if you would admit that the Divinity of Jesus Christ is - well, let us say, an exaggeration, we will grant you that He is the best guide to a decent life, and that if you follow His teaching you won't go far wrong. What more could you want than that? Into that kindly and amiable conversation the roll of the Christian drums breaks harshly - solemnly, the four big beats on the great drum first: 'God of God, Light of Light'; then it swells into a roar: 'Very God of Very God, Begotten not made, being of one substance with the Father, by Whom all things were made.' O my sacred aunt! says the world, this is ridiculous, it is not fair argument, it is not an argument at all, it is just very loud assertion. You cannot prove it, and so you take to shouting. That is how you win, because the man with a big voice always draws a crowd. But you cannot expect reasonable people to follow you, whatever the mob may do, and you'll lose the mob in the end; they'll start to think, you know, and then you will be in the soup. It's really no good shouting out a truth you cannot prove. You cannot prove that Jesus was 'His only Son,' and has a right to be 'our Lord,' the Lord of all the race. Now can you? No, I can't. I certainly can't, if by proof you mean a kind of coercive intellectual proof. There is no course of reasoning, however close and accurate, which can convince a man beyond all possibility of dispute that Jesus was not merely a good man among good men, a great teacher among great teachers, but God of God, Light of Light, Very God of Very God. I am convinced of that. If any one doubts the impossibility of that task, I would bid him get a good list of the books that have up to now been written on the subject of 'Christology,' and start in on them, and if he knows after the first hundred and fifty whether he's on his topsy or his turvy, then I'll be very much surprised. And they go on accumulating. Professor Jones replies to Professor Smith, and quotes the great authority Mr. Brown, then Bishop Jenkins butts in and bowls over the lot. What it all means, and where it all lands us, the God of mists and muddles alone knows, or can know. One has a ghastly sensation as one reads them that these books are mainly made up of a kind of glorified conjuring with great words.

The kind of certainty the Creeds express is not the kind of certainty that can be got by argument and reasoning. It can only be got by experience. Men can only come at it by accepting the challenge and betting their lives on it, living every day on the assumption that it is true, applying it carefully to problems as they arise, and seeing how the assumption works them out. But you must apply the assumption with your whole heart and soul, you must not wobble or waver on it, or it is no use. That is why the Creed accepts no compromise. What the man of the world really wants is to follow the teaching of Jesus when he likes and reject it as he chooses. He wants to accept the parts of it that seem reasonable and immediately practical, and reject what seems visionary and ridiculous, or even difficult. He wants to take Jesus as a human teacher whose teachings are expressions of his opinions, but nothing more. That sort of attitude is no use, says the Creed. You must either accept or reject the challenge, you cannot wobble; and if you are to do any good you must bet, you cannot wait and see whether it's a perfectly safe bet first. I cannot prove to you that it is bound to win. You must back the horse and ride it, ride it all out; and I say that as you feel its power beneath you, as you become conscious of its strength gathering with every stride, you will shout out your certainty as I shout mine, and will perceive the uselessness of arguments as a means to attaining certainty of this sort. We come back to that - the necessity of the great gamble. It is the same with all the big things of life; you have to bet, and you cannot bet on certainties. You have to take a risk.

All that reason can do is to show that there is not anything really irrational or absurd in the risk - that it is not pure lunacy. There is no peculiar virtue in being balmy. Life does demand that you should be brave, but it doesn't demand that you should make a silly fool of yourself. It does ask for faith, but it does not ask for folly.

But, you say, that is exactly what I feel this bet is - it is pure madness. It has got no sort of reason behind it at all. I simply cannot see why I should look at Jesus as God. In fact, I do not know what it means. But listen the point is, Do you think you should think of Him as Perfect Man, do you think that His Character stands out as the Ideal, the height of perfection to which we as a race are bound to attain in the end, and bound to strive after now? I'm not going to ask you, 'Do you love Jesus?' - it sounds the wrong sort of question, it has a sentimental touch about it; it ought not to have that, but it has. The point is, Are you ready to take Him as your Leader and your Guide - for better for worse, for richer for poorer, in sickness and in health, till death brings you closer to Him still? Are you willing to burn your boats behind you and declare for Jesus Christ as the Master and Captain of your fate? Never mind now whether He is God or man, human or Divine; that will come later, it is not the first step. The first step is to get fixed as to whether He is the Ideal after which in private and in public life, in matters of home, factory, or office, politics and international relations, you believe all men should strive. That is the first step, that always has been the first step - the surrender to Him as the great Ideal, the Perfect Man.

If you are not willing to surrender to Jesus as your Guide, you will never really know Him as your God, not even if you read arguments to prove it from now till you snuff out. If you are not willing to surrender to Him, then, as common sense man, you ought to ask, 'Why not?' You may say you don't need an ideal, and the world doesn't need an ideal, that you can muddle along without. And so you can, you can muddle along quite cheerfully perhaps, but you won't really live - you'll only play at it. You may say you know a better ideal, then for God's sake fork it out. I don't. I never came across any one in history who could pretend to stand in the same street with Him. I've said that before. It is no good talking about Jesus as God until, and unless, you take Him as Perfect Man. That is the kick-off to the Christian life. That is where we have been weak. We have been very strong on the fact that a man must accept the dogma of the

Divinity of Jesus in order to become a Christian, but we have not been half strong enough on the fact that he must first accept Him as Perfect Man, must adopt as his ideal His Character, with its hatred of lust, impurity even in thought, His detestation of revenge, hatred, pride, and selfishness. We must whole-heartedly accept the whole Jesus as our ideal. That is the real test of belief at the start. If you take it, you will find yourself up against the world at every turn, you will find yourself on the opposition bench to a very strong government. Your ideas of purity won't be the world's idea of purity. Your idea of marriage vows won't be the world's idea of marriage vows; when you make an oath you will really keep it, or count yourself as perjured. Your honesty won't be the world's honesty, and your idea of duty won't be the common idea of duty; you will find yourself 'up agin' it' in a thousand ways. And then your outlook upon yourself and your own character will not be the same; you will realise that you are a pretty average scoundrel, and that goodness is a big business. It will mean more to you when you say that Jesus was a 'good man.' You will begin to wonder whether a man who was just *human* in the same sense that you apply that adjective to yourself or your best pal could be 'good as Jesus was good,' whether a man who was sinless could be properly described as purely 'human' and nothing more. You never realise the difficulty of being 'good' until you start in and try to be good - not merely passable, but passionately good as Jesus was. Perhaps that does not sound attractive to you; you can't stand 'unco guid' people. Well, nor can I, nor can any one else; but that is because 'unco guid' people are not really good, but often repulsively bad. They are not charitable, they have not got the courage; they are not pitiful, they have not got the love; they are not saints, they are only Pharisees, and Pharisees were to Jesus like a bad smell. You cannot wriggle out of it that way. 'Goodness' in Jesus' sense has nothing to do with 'unco guidness'; it is as perfectly beautiful as it was in Him. When you set out to get it, to find the Holy Grail of spotless manhood or womanhood according to the pattern that Jesus wrought, you will very rapidly change your idea of what perfect humanity means, and it will dawn upon you that perfect humanity must be Divine, and Divine in a very real sense - a sense that stings, and hurts, and calls. The Divinity of Jesus to one who has set himself the task of attaining to goodness of His pattern ceases to be a dead dogma, and becomes a living, burning fact. I say you cannot get at its meaning by any other road than this road which He Himself called the way of the Cross: 'If any man would be My disciple, let him deny himself and take up his cross and follow after Me.' And there is more to it than that, because if you take Jesus as your Pattern Man, you must take Him as the Pattern Man for all men, you must endeavour to lead and persuade other men to set out on the same quest; you cannot be content to be good yourself and let all the world go hang. Goodness of the Jesus pattern is all mixed up with love, with giving what you have away. And when you start on that job of leading other men to follow the Perfect Man, you will become more and more impressed with the fact that you cannot do it - you cannot do it yourself. If it is to be done, He must do it - through you. You will come to it more and more - that you have nothing whatever to give away except the bit of His Spirit that you have caught; that unless you get out of the road and let Him come through, you have not a dog's chance of helping, comforting, or inspiring any one. This - these two results - inevitably follows the whole-hearted acceptance of Jesus as the Perfect Man. You come to realise first that you are utterly dependent on Him for your own goodness, and then that the world is utterly dependent on Him for its goodness - that is, goodness of His pattern. There is a lot of goodness among men that has nothing consciously to do with Him at all. Men are all the products of that queer process which is penetrated through with a Spirit whose purpose is the creation of the Human Family, and there is in them all a vein of nobility, generosity, tenderness, and honesty. You will recognise that - you cannot escape it - and if you are a Christian you will love it. Man as he is now is in many ways extraordinarily lovable. You would have to be a dull sort of fellow if you could fight with a British battalion and not get fond of the men. But if you had taken the first step, and taken Jesus as Perfect Man, you would be still more impressed with the fact that this goodness is not good enough, not nearly good enough, for the purpose of real brotherhood and real peace. It is utterly unreliable, it is subject to the most bewildering plunges into degradation, its purity is smutty, its honesty is wobbly, its selfishness is weakly, it has fine impulses but few big principles, it is purely human. You may say you love it, but you don't really; you don't love dirt, and smut, and lies, and meanness - you can't, they are so beastly ugly. The truth is that, good as men are, they are not good enough. They need - we need - another order of goodness altogether if the purpose of the world is to be realised and Man is to be created out of men. The Jesus pattern of goodness alone is good enough. His Life alone shows what has been working itself out through the process all the time, and shows it in human terms. The goodness of Jesus is the goodness of God, and is of another order from what can be called human goodness pure and simple. That is fundamentally what you mean when you call Jesus Christ 'His only Son our Lord.' That is the living dogma of the Divinity of Christ, and it is a faith that a man lives himself into after he has taken the first step of taking Jesus as Perfect Man. It is a truth that can only be grasped by the whole man, not by his intellect alone.

You have rejected the Divinity of Jesus up to now perhaps, because you felt it could not be intellectually proved, by reason, and that it was a truth which reason ought to be able to prove, and you were not going to be dishonest and say you believed when you were not convinced. I say that is all the wrong order. You cannot force or kill your intellect. Of course you can't, and you must not. Don't bother a tap about His Divinity as a dogma. The point you want to start with is His perfect humanity, the question you want to ask yourself is whether you ought to be like Him. Once you have fairly and squarely decided that, you have taken the first real step to prove that Jesus was Divine, that His goodness is the goodness of God, which all the travail of creation was undertaken to produce, the goodness that is good enough for real Brotherhood, real Socialism, real Peace on earth and Good Will amongst men.

Of course, your temptation will be to say that the goodness of Jesus is an impossible goodness - that it never can be yours or any one else's. Once you start trying it, you will not be likely to say that it is merely human; that is the kind of thing a scholar says who talks about it in the abstract, but is content with his own cleverness in the concrete. You will know it is Divine all right, but your temptation will be to say that it is impossible. If you reject it on these grounds - well, you know where you are, don't you? you know you are a coward who won't climb; you can't disguise yourself as an honest man who won't lie. But if you think fair and square on any big human problem, you will come to it that this impossible goodness is *necessary,* inevitable, if human dreams - the dreams of the Socialist, the Educationalist, the white man who loves his fellows - are to come true. This impossible goodness is necessary, is the very first necessity, if we are to make the better world, for the better world can only be made out of better men. The man who wants to make the world a better, happier place will come at last to see - if he is in earnest - that his heart's desire can only come true as this higher order of goodness is spread abroad in men's lives. If a man is going to be in dead earnest when he says -

'I will not rest from mental strife,
Nor sheathe the good sword in my hand,
Till we have built Jerusalem
In England's green and pleasant land,'

he will come at last to see that it can only be built on the foundation of that sort of goodness which is in Christ. He will come to see that the weak spot in all our schemes for betterment is human nature in its ordinary, wobbly, unreliable, good-and-evil state, and that on that rock our dreams are bound to suffer shipwreck soon or late. When you stand there with necessity behind you and impossibility in front, when the choice is stripped of all disguise and you see that it must be 'Christ or the present chaos,' then you are down on rock bottom, and will cry to the Perfect Man, 'Lord, I believe, help Thou mine unbelief - I do believe - I want to believe in Jesus Christ His only Son our Lord.'

VII. *Who was conceived of the Holy Ghost,* *Born of the Virgin Mary*

WE come to this. You cannot prove the truth of the Christian Creed by reading arguments in books, you must start out by doing actions in streets and factories and homes. The Christian Truth is not a matter of Truth and Falsehood only, it is a matter of Life and Death. Huxley was, of course, right when he said that the only question an honest man would ask was whether a doctrine was true or not, but he was wrong if he supposed that in all matters Truth could be attained by reasoning. The challenge of the highest Truth is not to the reason only, but to the whole man; at its heart the question of the Christian Faith is a moral one, a question of right and wrong. What Jesus did for the men of His time, what He does for the men of all time, is to hold up before them a new order of goodness, a fresh motive of life. He bids them seek and find 'Eternal Life,' a phrase which never meant to Him a kind of goldenharps-and-snow-white-wings-and-everlasting-hymns-before-the-great-white-throne existence, which was to come as a reward after death, but a new kind of life which was to begin here and now - at once. It was indeed never to find its completion and perfection in this world, but it was to begin here - begin in the honest and earnest search after that new order of goodness which Jesus showed to men as the goodness of God the Father.

If a man or woman honestly accepts that challenge, and sets out upon the quest of the Holy Grail of Jesus' goodness, he will begin to understand why Christians are so definite and determined about Jesus Christ as being 'His only begotten Son our Lord,' 'God of God, Light of Light, Very God of Very God,' et cetera. He will become convinced that to talk of a Person Who was the Author and actual example of this sort of goodness as being just a 'good man' is to use language without any real meaning. There never was a 'man,' however 'good,' who was like this. When you honestly start to live on this level, and stop arguing about it, you may come to the conclusion that Jesus' goodness is impossible, unpractical, visionary, mad, but you will not talk nonsense about its being 'merely human.' You may rail at it and Him as being inhuman and insane, and then His splendid wholesome sanity and His humanity in the best sense will stand up and ask you questions. He was a mad fanatic Who played with children. He was a morbid puritan Who declared war on natural instincts, and was called a glutton and wine-bibber and the friend of the harlots, Who forgave the woman taken in adultery. He was a ridiculous visionary with His eyes fixed on Heaven Who was always telling men that their first duty was to love one another and do good in this world. He was a megalomaniac madman Who was always talking about Himself as King of Heaven, and always thinking about other people, and living the simplest and humblest life of kindly service. He made Himself equal with God, and forgave the men that spit on His face. He was a weak and womanish pacifist Who could not strike an honest blow, Who faced a cross with the dignity of a hero, and died unbroken at the end. He was impossible, and infinitely appealing. If you set out to follow Him in earnest, you may say in your heart that He is 'the God of unbearable beauty Who breaks the hearts of men,' but you will cease to use the cant of the critic who calls Him a very good man.

> 'Yet take thou heed of Him, for, as thou pass
> Beneath this archway, then wilt thou become
> A thrall to His enchantments, for the King
> Will bind thee by such vows as is a shame
> A man should not be bound by, yet the which
> No man can keep, but, so thou dread to swear,
> Pass not beneath this gateway, but abide
> Without, among the cattle of the field.'

This is the vivid and bewildering spiritual experience that Christians have crystallised and summed up in the words 'His only Son our Lord,' the dogma of the Incarnation. They found His goodness perfectly beautiful, which means that they found it human in the best sense, calling on and pleading with all that was best and noblest in them, and at the same time they found it impossible and unattainable. They could not abandon it, it was too good; they could not attain to it, it was too high. He was at once inevitable and impossible, He was at once human and superhuman, He was God and man. That experience, which is at the root, and always has been at the root, of all vivid Christian Faith, would have been pure torture, had there not come with it the thrilling discovery that, impossible as He was, this Person was alive, alive and infectious; that though His goodness could not be taught or learned, it could be caught, and could catch you; and though it still remained beyond you, it could draw you towards it, and very slowly, and often painfully, transform you into its own image. The Jesus order of goodness is not only impossible and inevitable, it is also, thank God, infectious. This final experience completes the circle of enchantment by which Christ binds the souls of men and keeps them striving after the impossible, and still striving, though they fail a million times. This enchantment it is which is expressed in the dogma of Jesus Christ, the Saviour Who was God and Man, and which has made Christians ever since Christ died the laughing-stock and butt of all sensible and practical people, and has exposed them to charges of hypocrisy, folly, unreality, insincerity, morbidness, and all the hundred and one other curses that have been cast at them all through the many years that have been heaped upon the days of the Son of Man.

'Who that one moment hath the least described Him,
Dimly and faintly hidden and afar,
Doth not despise all excellence beside Him,
Pleasures and powers that are not and that are.

'Yea, amid all men bear himself thereafter,
Smit with a solemn and a sweet surprise,
Dumb to their scorn, and turning on their laughter
Only the dominance of earnest eyes.'

The dogma of the Incarnation is not a merely intellectual challenge, but a moral and spiritual one. It asks, 'Do you intend to abandon and give up the Christian standard of goodness because it is beyond you? ' and the Christian answer is given in the rolling of its unreasonable and idiotic but splendid drums, 'God of God, Light of Light, Very God of Very God, Begotten not made, being of one substance with the Father, by Whom all things were made.' No - No - No - I - won't - I will pass through the gateway; I will not abide without, among the cattle of the field.

This dilemma is not an artificial or merely intellectual dilemma, it is a terribly real and human one. The more one faces up to the facts of life, the more sternly one refuses to live in a blind fool's paradise, and determines to see life as it is, the clearer and more cogent grows the conviction that mankind must literally choose between Christ and the cattle of the field, between the higher order of goodness revealed in Jesus and pure animalism.

Nothing makes this issue clearer than the teaching of those who are opposed to Christ, deliberately and consciously opposed to His teaching. There are a large number of men and women who are deliberately opposed to Him, a larger number in Europe to-day than there has been for many generations. I have just been reading a book written by one of these teachers. It is difficult for me to say what I think of it and keep within the bounds of the English Dictionary, or outside the range of the laws of libel. But it does possess one great merit, it is honest and consistent. The author refuses to mince matters, and is determined to face facts. He gathers up all the scum and filth of modern civilisation and serves it hot as stinking soup. He hides nothing, and draws his picture with a heavy hand, and in very black ink. One reads it and grows sick. It is difficult indeed to believe it true and still retain one's faith in God. But then, of course, it is not true, it is one side of the truth. It is not a picture, because it is all shadow and no light. It is like a great deal of modern realism, which mistakes mere brutality for noble sincerity. Reading it, one would suppose that every man, woman, and child in the British Isles lives in a state of daily and hourly misery and degradation; that there is no laughter except the dirty sniggering of low-class music-hall audiences at obscene jokes; no honesty except when it is the best policy; no purity because all men are vicious and all women harlots at heart; no happiness because all men and women live in terror of starvation. You would suppose that a well-clad, well-nourished, happy-looking child is so rare as to be remarkable. It is a world of undiluted gloom - and yet this is a very poor and squalid quarter, where housing conditions are disgraceful, where the streets are mean and dirty, and the homes not fit for beasts, but the children of my schools who have just come out to play are shrieking with laughter, most of them are warmly clad, and their teachers love them (there is no class of public servants more honourable and less honoured than our elementary school teachers), and I love them, and they are not all unhappy or degraded; and this modern unrealist has a bee in his bonnet and a kink in his inside. He paints one side, the seamy side - but he does that faithfully. We cannot burke his truth, while we see his falsehood. There is a cesspool of undiluted cruelty and filth, on the edge of which our civilisation stands and staggers unsteadily. He says we are over the edge and into it, up to the neck, just sinking for the third time, and nothing can save us but the drastic and desperate course of drinking it - drinking it, stink, slime, and all. His way out is simple - simple, consistent, and logical, but, good Lord, it would choke an elephant. There are too many of us, he says, that is the root of the matter - there are too many of us, and we must get some of them killed off. In order to do this we must legalise and recognise as moral not merely prevention, but abortion and infanticide as well. Every mother and father must be left free to decide which of their new-born babes they shall kill and which they shall keep alive, the final decision resting with the mother. There is nothing, according to this teacher, but mawkish sentimentality and Christian hypocrisy to prevent this coming about quite soon. Women can be got to do anything that other women do, and they would take to murdering their babies as gaily as they have taken to short frocks, jazz dancing, and low-necked blouses. Men and women have no morals, only manners or conventions which depend mainly on their caprices and the climate. Once you set the ball rolling by the abolition of our present sentimental laws, they would keep it rolling, and the custom would be established in no time. They would soon realise, too, that half a husband is better than no husband at all, and free love without any vows other than a contract which could be terminated by mutual consent would solve the problems of the white-slave traffic and the unwanted woman at one stroke, and would also, which is of paramount importance, set men and women free to exercise their sex functions without artificial restraint or control. This would be the crowning blessing, because sexual control is at once impossible to attain and injurious to attempt. More than half our modern sickness, neurasthenia, madness, more than half our melancholies, jealousies, and perverted cruelties, are due to the unnatural suppression of the sex instinct. If you could somehow kill off, smother, and choke the pestilential Christian priest with his pink-passioned, pale-faced Christ, in whom he does not believe himself - for the Christian Religion is one part folly and three parts humbug - you would then be free to live according to the true creed, which is that man is an animal which has happened, by circumstances over which it has no control, to have its brain specially developed as it might have had its forelimbs turned into wings, claws, suckers, or some other of the thousand forms which nature bestows. Once we start to live natural animal lives, all the troubles of our artificial civilisation will pass away. Our one great need is the honesty and courage to face the fact that we are what we are - beasts that perish. There is the solution: get rid of the King and His enchantments, and be content to abide without, among the cattle of the field.

There you have the dilemma, stark-naked and stripped of all disguise; and the only difference between this particular book and countless others of the same sort is that stark-nakedness and freedom from disguise. The same teaching in a milder form is being poured out upon the children of this generation, and is more dangerous, like all other lies, when it wears a Sunday suit borrowed from the angels of beauty and of truth. The teachers of it are largely followers of Freud, the psychologist, who have never read his books, and dabblers in psycho-analysis with the most elementary sort of knowledge of what it all means. It is a ghastly thing for one who has studied and come to understand the powers of suggestion to contemplate the unnatural alliance which has been formed between the specialist in his study and the fool in every street to debauch the minds of the people with a flood of new sex teaching.

The scientific specialist who spends his life in the investigation and treatment of obscure nervous disorders sets out his tentative and very imperfect discoveries, which are hailed immediately as universally established facts, and exploited by a host of eagerly ignorant people who have neither the ability nor the patience to test their truth or falsehood. Freud doubtless performed a great service to humanity when he disclosed the enormous part which the sub-conscious mind plays in determining our daily actions. He was undoubtedly right when he resolved that no prejudice and ignorant opposition should prevent him from revealing the power of the sex instinct in man's sub-conscious life. He was and is right in maintaining that sex desire is the most powerful factor in ordinary human nature, and that the unnatural and forcible suppression of sex desire by the will in obedience to convention or fear of consequences is the cause of frequent mental and moral disasters. In all this he was right, but his followers have been damnably and disastrously wrong in supposing that the only outlet for this powerful desire, and the only way of preventing its unnatural suppression, is to increase our freedom of sexual intercourse. The sex instinct has only one outlet in animals, but it has a thousand and one in men. Every creative, artistic, and religious faculty man possesses is a development of what Freud calls sex instinct, and all man's social, poetic, and religious activity is an outlet

- and *the proper human outlet* - for it. We have here one of the usual 'scientific' errors arising out of the ridiculous habit of looking for the explanation of things in their origins. These teachers will tell you that because the religious instinct is connected with the sex instinct, and is undoubtedly a development of it, therefore the religious instinct is only the sex instinct disguised, with a veneer over it, and the love of a noble Christian woman for Christ is only a perversion of the love which should have found its natural satisfaction in intercourse. They will tell you with contempt that a woman only worships God when she cannot get a husband. It is only one branch, and a very important branch, of the deep-seated error into which the so-called scientific method has led thinkers for more than a century. It is the old business which declares that because I am descended from a monkey, therefore I am only a monkey, and tries to get the world to progress looking backwards. All this teaching which makes man the inevitable slave of a tyrannous sex craving for which no outlet is possible but the 'natural' one, which says that purity is impossible and therefore we must have polygamy, that restraint is impossible and therefore we must have infanticide, abortion, and prevention as cures for over-population, is intellectually based upon the fundamental error of finding the meaning of the end in the beginning. But that is not the root of it; the root of it is a moral refusal to accept the struggle for existence which every higher form of life must make if it is to survive. It proceeds from that desire for lower peace and contentment, that harmony of the lower level, which is the temptation of all living things, and which ends in extinction and death. Every new form of life has to struggle for its existence or die, and that struggle is the eternal method of progress. Life-force, which is another name for God, seeks ever for new outlets; it broke through matter and issued in mind, and it must break through mind into something higher still. In this matter of sex the tremendous force behind instinct has broken through and found for itself many new outlets in man; it has broken into art, music, poetry, literature, invention, and scores of other channels, but most of all, it breaks through into religion, and finds an outlet into the infinite and eternal.

The connection between religion and sex is undoubted and undisputable, but the meaning of the beginning is found in the end, not vice versa. The meaning of sexual connection is to be found in spiritual union, in love - true love. It is love that explains lust, not lust that explains love. Love is the new and higher life that has to struggle for its existence. These teachers deny its existence, and give its name to lust, denying that there is anything else. The struggle is irksome, socially and individually irksome, and they will not take it up. This teaching is the teaching of death. Literally, and in so many words, it is the everlasting call of the waters of Lethe - to sleep and forget, and be content; it is the call of decadence - to take the way down as the way out; and the call is loudest in this question of sex. Here is the very heart of the struggle. Abandon the battle at this point, and you must retreat all along the line. Here it is that in the life of each man and woman, and in the life of every community, the struggle is hardest and most painful. Frequently it amounts to torture, and ends in madness or in suicide, frequently, too, in obscure nervous complaints, obsessions, melancholies, down-right madness. There is no doubt about those facts. There is no doubt, too, that many teachers, preachers, and social workers, who have the highest aims, and are altogether on the right road in other ways, make hideous mistakes because they do not understand the struggle and its sorrows fully, and do not show the right way out. They are content to say that lust is sin, and leave the wretched man or woman to fight it by the power of their already broken will - a hopeless task indeed. There is no doubt that the teaching of the Church on the matter of sex has been, and often is still, marred by ignorance, stupidity, and cowardice.

But it is into this very centre of the struggle for the higher goodness that the Creed comes marching with its drums. It adds to the words 'Jesus Christ His only begotten Son our Lord,' the words, 'Who was conceived of the Holy Ghost, born of the Virgin Mary.' It asserts violently that the higher order of goodness which came with Jesus came in a unique way, and a way which delivered it from any contamination by lust. It was an order of goodness which set love free from lust and so made it perfect. This doctrine is the point on which the 'natural' school of sex teaching concentrate all their powers of abuse, ridicule, and contempt. It has been laughed at, mocked at, and covered with decent and indecent contempt for centuries, and most of all during the great scientific century. It is offensive to the natural school, not only because it is miraculous, but because it has led to the belief in love as distinct from natural lust, a distinction which they abhor.

It is true that in their desperate loyalty to love Christians went too far, and looked upon virginity and celibacy as the higher life, and tended to regard all sex connection as, if not sinful, at any rate a lower kind of good. This was the result of its passionate rejection of the lower goodness, and its determination to seek love unstained by lust. Even an opponent, and a contemptuous opponent, of Christianity like Mr. Edward Carpenter admits that Christianity represented the most powerful reaction against the long, intolerable tyranny of the senses over the soul. And it still remains the most powerful rebel against that tyranny, and it is this fierce rebellion that has its power-centre in the doctrine of the Virgin Birth. All the Christian belief in the purity of womanhood, the sacredness of motherhood, the beauty of home life, centres round the Holy Family, and especially round the infinitely gracious and appealing figure of Our Lady. All the Christian belief in romance as opposed to mere sex adventure, in love which means self-sacrifice, in child-bearing as a sacred vocation, gathers itself around the manger and the stable.

'Come sail with me o'er the golden sea
To the land where the rainbow ends,
Where the rainbow ends,
And the great earth bends
To the weight of the starry sky,
Where tempests die with a last fierce cry,
And never a wind is wild.
There's a Mother mild, with a little Child
Like a star set on her knee,
Then bow you down, give Him the crown,
'Tis the Lord of the world you see.'

Perversions, degradations, and inconsistencies have marred its appeal and corrupted its teaching, but that picture still remains as the power-centre of Christian purity. And it is as such, as the power-centre of the Christian protest against lust, that it stands, and always has stood, in the Christian Creed. It was because they accepted the Jesus standard of goodness, which demanded purity, not merely in deed but in thought, and separated love utterly from lust, that it seemed almost natural and inevitable to them that He should be Virgin born. It is because I accept the Jesus standard of goodness - accept it, God help me! even in this matter of purity - that I cannot be certain that the miracle did not happen. When I say in the Creed 'conceived of the Holy Ghost, born of the Virgin Mary,' it means primarily that I believe in and accept with all my heart the Jesus standard of purity as the ideal to which I must attain. I believe in the Holy Family and all it stands for. I believe in the redemption of lust, and its transformation into faithful loyal love to God and man. I take the road up, the struggle and the Cross, and I reject the road down, as the way out of my present sorrows, and the sorrows of the world about me. And because I have tried to reach that standard, tried and failed, and keep on failing, because there is in me

'That underworld where lust and lies
Like vermin crawl and creep
Across my visions and my prayers
Whence sordid passions leap

'To slay the very thing I love,
To crucify my Lord,
And force me spit my sins upon
The face my soul adored,'

because I know the intense and appalling difficulty of that road up, and yet have known with a thrill that there is redemption in Jesus' goodness, and that He has power with this lie of lust, that He can break its grip and lift me up, it is because of that experience that I cannot suppose that Jesus' goodness is purely human goodness, or that Jesus was just a good man. I never knew a man, however good, who had not fought and failed at times, and so I am driven to suppose either that He was a myth or a unique and superhuman personality. I cannot accept the mythical Jesus - its invention would be a greater miracle than His reality - and I am driven to accept His reality as a unique and superhuman personality; and then, with that background, I have to face the question, Did the miracle happen or not? With that background, mind you, with that background I am still doubtful whether it did occur, without it I would be perfectly certain it did not. I believe in the miracle, so far as I do believe in it, because of Jesus. I do not believe in Jesus because of the miracle. I am bound to be sceptical about miracles. Scepticism in its proper place is just as necessary, and just as much a duty, as faith. I must not, and cannot, accept any story that I would like to be true, nor must you. Intellectual honesty in matters where the intellect applies is just as necessary a virtue as the honesty which forbids you to steal your neighbour's Sunday boots. And to a certain extent the intellect does apply to this matter. Either this thing happened or it did not, and we have to weigh up the evidence for and against. It is a dreary business. It has been done again and again by different men, who arrived at different conclusions because their bias of mind gave them a different background. It seems to me that this must always be. The historical evidence is not conclusive either way. It leads, and must lead, to a verdict of not proven. The evidence is as good as it could possibly be for such an event, which, when it occurred, could not possibly have been known to more than two persons - St. Joseph and the Blessed Virgin Mary herself - both of whom have apparently left records, the one in St. Matthew and the other in St. Luke. The records are different in detail, but agree in the main fact. There is no conclusive evidence that either St. John or St. Paul knew about it, but then neither is there any compelling proof that they didn't. It is a bewildering problem, and I feel sure that the study of the historical evidence, unless some more is discovered, cannot lead to any positive certainty either way. I do not think it was put into the Christian Creed because of the historical evidence for it. Nor do I believe it was put in because it was a fulfilment of Jewish prophecy, or regarded as such. I do not think it was just a desire to pile up miracles. Christians do not display a tendency to record any sort of miracle for the sake of inspiring wonder, and the evangelists have left on record our Lord's reluctance to prove His authority by performing signs and wonders. I think it found its place in the Creed and has kept it because the purity of Jesus seemed to His followers to demand such a miracle - *a unique personality demanded a unique birth*. And the religious significance, the actual call of this clause in the challenge, is to accept that standard of purity which was in Jesus as the Divine Ideal for men and women; and to that call I respond, and believe that men and women must respond, if we are to find a way out of our many sorrows, and found the better world.

But because I do accept, and cannot help accepting, the uniqueness of the Character of Jesus, it does make my outlook different, and I cannot be sure that the miracle did not happen. To begin with, of course, I take it that it is tolerably clear nowadays that a man who denies the possibility of any miracle having ever happened, or of any miracle ever happening in the future, is rather a ridiculous person, thirty years behind the times, who is really claiming omniscience, and pretending that he is intimately acquainted with all the hidden and mysterious resources of the universe. It is possible to show that the dogmatic materialist has made a fool of himself in this matter before now, and denied the possibility of things which have actually occurred. A study of the evidence for the cure of disease by spiritual healing, hypnotic suggestion, auto-suggestion, and other kindred methods would make it clear that it is far too early to make dogmatic assertions of possibility or impossibility where the relation of mind to matter and of body to soul is concerned.

You may, of course, grant that it is difficult to imagine the Creative Power breaking or suspending the action of His own laws, and then point out that it is perfectly possible for a human intelligence who knows the laws of nature, by combining and observing, without breaking, them, to produce results which to a person without his knowledge would appear to be stark-naked miracles. Thus I suppose telegraphy, telephony, and wireless communication would appear to a savage to be miraculous; and the idea of lighting his bathroom and heating his bathwater with lightning would have appeared wildly improbable to my great-grandfather. And if it is possible for a human intelligence to thus combine and submit to nature's laws, and produce 'miracles' for the savage, it is much more possible for the Intelligence Who made the human intelligence to combine without breaking His own laws in such a way as to produce miracles that would baffle the best of us for all time.

But when you have granted all this, the fact remains that the uniformity of nature's working, *i. e.* of God's working in nature, has been proved to be such a true assumption that any apparent break in it has to be viewed with suspicion. We cannot admit the probability of a break occurring without very special reasons to account for it, and then we do not think of it as a real break, but as a new combination of forces. We cannot admit the probability of God's continual interference with laws of nature; or else we lose our sense of the reliability of the universe as a whole, which is the foundation upon which our ordinary lives are built, and which is to the religious man very precious as the Faithfulness of God.

But for *a very special reason* we may rationally admit the probability of an apparent break. There have certainly been in the past two such apparent breaks, two events which are still, as far as we know, stark-naked miracles: one was the emergence of organic out of inorganic matter, and the other the emergence of mind out of matter. At these two crises in history there were breaks. Now, if the Birth of Jesus was another such crisis in history, and if the Birth of Jesus meant not merely the birth of another man, but the birth of a new race - the birth of Man, the Human Unity, Brotherhood; if Jesus was unique, as I believe Him to be, then there is a very special reason for the apparent break, and the Virgin Birth becomes credible - against that background. The objection that this puts Christ further away and makes Him inhuman does not hold. It draws Him nearer, as near as in experience Christians have found Him to be. If Jesus was merely a freak man - a genius - then I have no more hope of being good as He was good than I have of writing plays as Shakespeare wrote plays. No one is so utterly aloof from ordinary humanity as the genius. But if in Jesus a new break was made by God and life-force shot up higher, as it did when Life and when Mind appeared, and if I can become partaker of that Life, as experience tells me I can to a very limited extent, then there is infinite hope, and I can say, 'Brethren, now are we the sons of God, and it does not yet appear what we shall be, but we know that when He shall appear we shall be like Him, for we shall see Him as He is.'

The attempts of Christians to be Christian now are almost as ridiculous as the attempts of the first men to be human, but it is not for us who have had such strange beginnings to despise the day of small things. Contempt generally means stupidity and lack of imagination, and it certainly does in this case. Eternal Life on earth is still in its infant stage - only two thousand years old, and what is that in time's eternity of time? As individuals and as a race we are only children, and there is much ahead. Against this background the Virgin Birth seems possible or even probable, and Our Lady dons her robes again. But I do not really think that her robes of sweet purity and love depend upon the actual occurrence of the physical miracle. By whatever means that glorious Character was born into the world, she is still the Mother of Christian mothers, and one among ten thousand. She still sits by her Manger or stands by her Cross and calls out to the world of men and women her challenge to the flesh in the name of the Spirit, calling us to pass beneath the gateway of Christ's purity and leave the life of the cattle in the field. And if a man will take up the challenge honestly and sincerely, and set out to seek the Holy Grail, I believe he can say his Creed in the spirit, even if for honesty's sake he has to remain uncertain that the miracle occurred.

This much, at any rate, is certain, that the miracle will remain ludicrous and incredible to those who refuse the challenge and make no effort to subdue the flesh to the Spirit, and no amount of evidence could ever convince them of its truth. The real question at issue is not an intellectual but a moral one, and I firmly believe that the Creed of the Virgin Birth is practically the only one in which there is any hope of salvation from our present miseries. We cannot go back to the beasts even if we would. Christ has been too long in the world, and has accomplished too much. He may have to be crucified afresh, but He will rise again. There is no way out of the tyranny of lust save the way that leads upwards unto love.

I do not believe that what is called the 'new sex' teaching, which in its essence is as old as savagery, has any future. The race that adopts it will commit suicide. I know that the struggle for purity is agony very often. I know that it causes misery, and has the appearance of hypocrisy, forcing men to profess what they do not practise, but so does the higher life all round, and I do not believe that there is any real escape backwards; we must go forward and upward, by the agelong way of the Cross. And it has its compensations and consolations. It humiliates you, wounds you, makes you feel a hypocrite and a fraud, but it leads to clean manhood, clean womanhood, and Christian self-respect. The sex instinct is only really tyrannous when you stunt its growth upward and outward, and prevent its flowering into poetry, art, music, and into communion with the Eternal God. This ancient and modern doctrine that it is better not to marry in order that you may continue to burn, because burning with lust is the only real joy in life, may have its hot-house pleasures and its thrills, but it leads at last to would-be-young old men and women, with no hope in front and no pride behind, trying to keep alive the thrills of youth, undignified and indecent remains. It is founded on a lie, and it makes life a mean scramble for passing pleasures, with no real romance, no heroism, no self-sacrifice in it. Thousands are living the life to-day, as thousands have lived it for centuries, with no shame and no attempt at restraint, and they are not good advertisements for it. I know I shall be told that the corruption and degradation which follow on that kind of life to-day, the bestial excess, the disease, the callousness, are all the result of the wicked Christian conspiracy, and that if you set men and women perfectly free, they would be as innocent and unconscious of wrong in promiscuous intercourse as dogs are, that they would kill their babes with tender hearts, and change their mates innocently as often as they felt inclined, that they would no longer be prurient and absorbed in sex once you killed all the men with black coats and preposterous collars, but that talk is pure bosh. The idea that if you set men free from all restraint, and from the fetters of convention, they will become naturally moderate and decent people who will treat their women kindly and sacrifice their passions to their highest welfare, has about as little real evidence to rest upon as any lie I know. Everything we know of human nature is against it. This idea of freedom is a caricature. I am a 'free' man when I sit down to a piano; I am bound by no law, and subject to no conventions, and I produce the most horrible and brain-splitting results. The real musician is a slave, bound by iron laws and fettered by complex conventions, but he produces music that the angels stoop to hear. If man is to produce the music of eternal life he must be bound by the laws of the master musician, and be subject to the conventions of Christ; he must be a slave in that service which is perfect freedom.

The real reason why the sex life of our people runs into vice and consequent mental and physical disease is not the pressure upon their lives of Christian conventions and laws of purity, but the fact that for most of them the proper human outlets for the great desire are dammed up. They have no real art, only moving pictures; they do no creative work, they only mind machines - they produce much but create nothing; they have no music but jazz dances; and, to our shame, my shame, they have no religion, and cannot find their way out into the eternal - they are spirits in prison. The proper outlets upward are dammed, and they seek the outlet downwards, and that is not an outlet at all, but a rotten road that is not a thoroughfare. And these spirits in prison are exploited for money wholesale by novelists, playwrights, pressmen, picture-postcard venders; the exploitation of pruriency is one of the most paying businesses in the world. Lust pays enormous dividends. It is a sure thing, a dead cert, and a damnable disgrace. So Mammon and Venus join hands and persecute the Christ; but, in spite of all their apparent power, I believe the future lies with Him, with Him and the Virgin of Bethlehem. I believe that the race will turn at last to the Mother Maid and to the Child upon her knee, finding in Him the way upwards and the way out.

VIII. *Suffered under Pontius Pilate*

IF you get down to the bottom of it, you will often find that the difference between two men who argue quite rationally about something is not really a rational difference at all, but an instinctive one. Both men will argue quite reasonably, and will appeal to evidence in support of their particular attitude, and both will firmly believe that they are perfectly reasonable people who approach the subject without prejudice, and with completely open minds, but underneath all the reasons there are instinctive forces at work which really influence their judgment, and force them almost to select the kind of evidence that appeals to them. At bottom it is a matter of taste.

That sounds rather a hopeless outlook, because it is popularly supposed that there is no good arguing on matters of taste, it is waste of time. If a man does not like rice pudding or Watts' pictures, there is no good proving to him that he really does. He does not, and there is an end of it. But the case is not really so desperate as that, for, although you cannot argue your friend Williams into a taste for Watts, you may argue him into studying Watts for himself, and so acquiring a taste for him. You may not be able to prove to your son Philip that he loves rice pudding, but you may persuade him to try it, and acquire a taste for it. Any number of tastes are not natural but acquired, and often acquired with some difficulty. You may be able to persuade a man to give something a trial - to take the plunge, make the venture, give the thing a fair chance, and so acquire a taste for it. But it is important to realise the nature of the difficulty you are up against in an argument, to uncover the instinctive prejudice that sways your opponent's mind, and allow for prejudices that may be swaying yours. It is important to realise that an unbiased mind, if it is a possibility, is the rarest thing on earth. We are not nearly as rational as we seem. We act and judge on impulse, and then find reasons for the action and judgment afterwards.

There is no doubt that to most men and women Christ is an acquired taste, hardly ever a natural one. The natural man has an instinctive repulsion from Him, and it is very often this instinctive repulsion, and not any rational difficulty, that keeps him from being a Christian, although he himself would tell you that it is purely intellectual doubt that stands in the way. But you will find that until the instinctive repulsion is met with and overcome the strongest arguments will fall fiat, and all the flatter because the man thinks that he is perfectly rational, when underneath him all the time the hidden forces of instinct are at work.

Sometimes it is good instinct, and sometimes it is a rotten bad one. You reason with a man for hours, and he replies with apparent sincerity of doubt and difficulty of a reasonable sort, and then you discover that he is a secret sensualist and means to stick to it, or is suffering from acute intellectualitis and worships his own brain, and you know that you might as well argue with a donkey about its unreasonably long ears - unless you get down to tin-tacks and tackle the real issue.

One of the strongest and most deeply-seated instincts that sway normal men is repulsion from pain and suffering. It is a natural repulsion with a very obvious purpose, and intensely strong, and strongest in the healthiest people. If a man likes inflicting pain, or desires to endure it, and there are heaps of men and women who do, healthy-minded people agree that he is either mad or bad, or both. Yet one of the strongest impressions that Christ made upon the men of His own time, and one of the strongest impressions He makes upon the men of to-day, is the impression of His sufferings. He was, and is, seen to be 'a man of sorrows and acquainted with grief.' And His Gospel has often been stated, and is still often stated, in such a way as to glorify suffering as a good thing, sent by God, and give the impression that Christ taught, and would have us believe, that pain and suffering were good things, and that a man who suffered was to be admired and reverenced for it whether He suffered for any good purpose or not. Christians themselves have often been morbid people, and believed that suffering of any sort was the Will of God, and always tended to purge the soul and make for purity of heart. We all know the kind of Christian who manufactures his own crosses by the dozen, and then pathetically claims your admiration for the way he bears them; the morbid hysterical woman who walks the way of sorrows paved by her own distorted and self-centred imagination with the air of a saintly martyr done to death for truth. We all know these people, and they are the despair of our lives, for there is no more soul-destroying evil than self-pity that mistakes itself for sacrifice.

If we are to have healthy minds and live healthy lives, we must assume quite definitely and clearly that pain and suffering are evil things, and that to endure them without necessity is folly, and the most futile of all follies, and to inflict them without necessity is sin, and the most sinful of all sins. There is no sin so vile and so degrading as deliberate cruelty, and the essence of cruelty is the infliction of unnecessary pain. We cannot be too definite about the sinfulness of cruelty of any sort whatever. But we must also recognise that, evil as pain and suffering are, they are by no means the worst of evils, and that to endure them *for a good and sufficient reason* is the highest wisdom, and to inflict them with *a good and sufficient purpose* is the most perfect kindness. Only the purpose must be good and sufficient. We must have a perfectly good object, and we must make absolutely certain, as far as we humanly can, that we cannot possibly attain that object without inflicting suffering and pain. That sounds like rather ponderous and platitudinous (those words have an imposing appearance, haven't they? - just like fat men with loud voices) common sense; but the most ghastly sorrows have been endured by men and women, and especially children, because the truth was not recognised and good religious people looked upon pain and suffering as good things which it was always beneficial to inflict and endure, and which always tended to purge and purify the heart. They have been convinced that men could only be saved from sin by suffering, and that God sent suffering into the world for that good purpose. This idea has led Christians to tolerate and regard as inevitable a great deal of totally unnecessary and avoidable suffering. It has led them to condone and even regard as beneficial ghastly social conditions, involving the daily torture of men and women. It has enabled them to contemplate a dirty, unorganised, wasteful, and stupid world as God's appointed place of preparation for the next. The Church has given its blessing to a stupid and cruel chaos on the ground that it was God's appointed preparation for a wondrous order after death. Only the other day a good Christian was telling me of some outdoor services in a poor quarter, and described with great satisfaction the crowd of dirty, unkempt, and degraded-looking people that thronged around the preacher. He was delighted with the service. Here was the real thing, the preaching of the Gospel to God's poor. So picturesque and romantic. It did not strike him that the existence of such people and their miserable pig-sty houses was a reproach to the Gospel and a wound in the heart of Christ. Of course, when he was challenged with it, he saw it, *but he had to be challenged.* He had to be shaken out of his piety into practical humanity. It was necessary to make him, a good Christian man, see that this stupid and avoidable suffering was a sin. He was still under the spell of that perversion of Christ's Gospel which leads to the sinful and morbid glorification and sentimentalising of stupid cruelty. The same attitude has been commonly taken by Christians towards disease. It was God's chastening, to be meekly accepted and submitted to. It was the cup of suffering given by the Father, and must be drunk to the dregs. It was a special privilege to be allowed to share Christ's sufferings, and the sufferer must look upon it as such. These things are sent by a watchful Providence to test and try us. So in a vicious circle the morbid lie worked round, fastening the chains of sorrow tighter round man's hands and feet. Cruelty walked proudly round the streets arrayed in the shining robes of Christ. The error is fatal because it disguises cruelty and gives it a religious sanction, and that is the very thing sin always seeks - a good disguise. Again and again men have tortured their fellows in the name of God, pretending that it was for their own good, and deceiving themselves, when really it was the morbid and savage love of inflicting pain that was urging them on. 'See thou to what damned deeds religion draweth men' is as true of the Christian religion as any other. Men have found doctrines to disguise and cover the bestial cruelty and vindictiveness of their own natures. There is no doubt that much of the powerful appeal which the teaching of the Divine frightfulness and eternal punishment had for the elect was due to the freedom it gave them to revel in thought over the vengeance which they could not inflict themselves, but which God would inflict for them upon their enemies. It was due to the making of God in man's image, and the picturing of God's justice as being like our degraded and makeshift justice.

Few words have been so misused as 'Justice.' Justice has been supposed to demand that a sinner should suffer whether any good purpose was served by the suffering or not. He 'deserves' to suffer, and that is enough. Nine men out of ten do not know what the word 'deserve' means. It is a word that covers a multitude of sins - like charity. It covers up any Lord's quantity of vindictiveness, and cruelty, and callousness. The truth is, that no one deserves a pang of pain unless it is necessary for his own good, or the good of other men, unless it serves a purpose which cannot be otherwise accomplished. This idea of 'Justice' as something distinct from Love has been a curse to the world. Even now our prisons are full of men and women who 'deserved' to suffer, and who will be all the worse for it, and all the greater danger to society because of it, and several steps nearer Hell than they were before they suffered. Suffering was inflicted on them in the name of 'Justice' because we were too lazy, too ignorant, and too stupid to get to the root of their sin and save them from it. The history of this world's courts of 'Justice' would turn a strong man sick. All through time man, with his genius for self-deception and hypocrisy, has dressed up his sin in the robes of this attribute of God, and then fallen down and worshipped it. The really just man is the man who inflicts and permits only absolutely necessary pain, and *who suffers himself in doing so*. The more perfectly just a man is, the more he will strive to avoid inflicting pain, and the more keenly he will suffer himself when he has to inflict it - of necessity. God's justice must mean an infinity of effort to avoid inflicting or permitting pain and suffering, and an infinity of sorrow to Himself when He has to permit or inflict it - of necessity. God's justice is God's Love.

If justice means the rationing out of pain and pleasure to people as they 'deserve' it, this world is not just at all. Pain is not distributed according to desert in this world. Looking for that sort of justice in life is like looking for a needle in a haystack when it is not there. The best people suffer most again and again. Life is not fair, and cannot be made fair, except on the surface, and that with great difficulty. It is true that we can remedy, and must remedy, the glaring surface 'injustices' of life, the disgusting extremes of riches and poverty, the ridiculous differences of opportunity for education and development, but these are only surface injustices, and when we have remedied them all, life will not be fair. And in our effort to remedy them we shall discover, and do, that our greatest enemy is this idea of desert. People who have been given by God greater brain-power and higher ability look upon themselves as deserving all they can get, and as being in some mysterious way better than the common ruck of men. They have a right to affluence while others starve.

They deserve to live in fine houses with large gardens and a tradesman's entrance while others pig it two families in one room. They deserve these blessings. Under that blessed notion they disguise their selfishness. And it is all a pack of stupid nonsense. They don't deserve anything, and are not a ha'porth better than any decent man who earns £3 per week, and often not as good. They were given these gifts of brain and ability to serve and help with, they were given them as *trusts* for a noble purpose, and unless they fulfil the trust, they are just common thieves. There is no desert about it.

And when you have killed that lie and remedied the surface injustices, you will not have made the world fair. Still the natural gifts which make for pain or pleasure are unequally distributed without any attention to desert. Brains, beauty, charm, genius are not distributed according to desert, and they are treasures beyond the power of money to buy. Of course, in the orthodox religious scheme of things beauty and charm do not count, they are only skin deep, but as a matter of fact they are the most coveted gifts in the world, and productive of intense pleasure, and are tremendous powers for good or evil. There is no greater devil than a beautiful and charming devil, and no saint so powerful as a charming saint. They are distributed unequally, and with no attention to desert. Stupidity, awkwardness, shyness are not distributed equally, or as they are deserved, and they are the cause of agonies. Misfortunes, accidents, disease, and death are not sent to those that deserve them. What is the use of pretending that they are? You may be a saint, but that will not prevent you from falling down the cellar steps and breaking your leg. Life does not always punish the guilty and reward the innocent. The Jews tried hard to believe that it did, but it only broke their hearts, and it will break the heart of any one who tries to believe it, unless he is the kind of person who can see a hundred children burned to death and thank God they were not his, or hear that a battalion of fine men has been cut to pieces and thank God he was not there. That kind of gratitude to the Almighty is fairly common, and I often wonder what He thinks of it. An exceptionally fortunate person might persuade himself of the idea that the world was just, provided he never felt the truth -

> 'That loss is common does not make
> My loss the less but rather more.
> Never morning wore
> To evening but some heart did break.'

It is not true that if you are good you will escape pain, or that if you are sinful you will incur it. The better you are the more pain you may be called upon to endure, and the worse you are the more pleasure you may manage to obtain. I know of no task more hopeless than the endeavour to maintain that God's government of this world is just in the sense of awarding reward and punishment according to desert. When you get down beneath the surface into the underworld of private hopes and fears and horrors, where the real tragedies of life are played out, and have laid bare before you the tortures which good men and women suffer, and when you know with what brutality the law of heredity works out, this copy-book lie about the way to happiness being goodness, and the way to sorrow sin, turns you sick. It is just soothing syrup and untruth. God is not just in that sense of the word. This world is not a complete, finished, and justly ordered place where all things happen as they should, where all the good little boys get halfpennies and all the bad little boys get smacks. If belief in God depended upon maintaining the truth of that lie, then belief in God were impossible.

But belief in God does not depend upon it. The Christian religion starts off by aiming a blow at that lie. That is its chiefest glory. It begins with the best Man that ever lived hanging in agony on a Cross, and so faces up to facts right away. There is its splendour. It is rooted in the most stark-naked act of injustice that the mind could well conceive. There stands Perfect Man, with the spittle of a drunken soldier streaming down His face, a crown of thorns set sideways on His head, with blood from the great wounds in His back sousing red through the dirty purple cloth that mockery has thrown across His nakedness - there stands Christ. Behold the Man! All history is summed up in that scene. There is no truer picture of what history reveals than a Crucifix. As it stood in a broken Flanders village, looked up to by broken bleeding men, as it stands in some rotten slum to-day while the squalid crowd pass seething by, it is the Truth - the Martyrdom of God in Man. Life is as brutal as it is brutal, as repulsive as it is repulsive, as unjust as it is unjust, and, thank God, as perfectly beautiful as He is perfectly beautiful. That is the secret. The Cross is not God's Will, but God's Woe. The Christ is God's Will - He is perfect Beauty. But His beauty is not for all to see. To many there is no beauty that they should desire Him. They cannot see Christ for the Cross. It stands in the way. It blots Him out. They have been taught, perhaps, that the Cross was God's plan, that God willed it; it was part of His scheme, and they are repelled. What a God! What a plan!

They would be prepared to admire Christ for His sufferings if they could see any good and sufficient reason for them. 'This have I done for thee; what wilt thou do for Me?' pleads the preacher. 'What hast Thou done for me?' answers the man in the street. 'What purpose did this suffering serve?' 'It saved the world from sin,' says the preacher, 'But it didn't,' says the man in the street, 'you know it didn't. You are talking cant - pious cant. It didn't save the world from sin. Sin and sorrow still continue, misery and wretchedness are with us yet, and fall like the rain upon the just and the unjust too. Men still torture men and women, children still go hungry, there is still rape and murder, lust and war. Our streets are full of it, our papers ring with it, the world remains unsaved, and the heaviest burdens still fall upon the best of men. Calvary made no difference. It is a summary of life's problem, but not a solution.'

'But Salvation is possible now,' says the preacher; 'it was impossible before. Man can now be saved from sin. God's justice has been satisfied. You see, God's justice required that man must suffer for his sin, his rebellion against God, before he could be forgiven. All the world would, by the law of justice, have been doomed to eternal torment in an everlasting Hell if Jesus had not suffered and saved us from that awful fate. God could not forgive, even if man repented, unless the law of justice were satisfied and the punishment which sin deserved was borne by man in Christ. You do not understand the awful Holiness of God.' But the man in the street gets frantic here. 'No, I don't,' he says, 'and I don't want to. I don't want to understand a justice that demands eternal agony for three-score years and ten of ignorance, sorrow, and sin. Who is this just God? I do not believe there is such a Being. If there is, He must be the Devil. If I could meet Him, I would tell Him what I thought of His justice even if I went to Hell for it afterwards. Justice which demands eternal punishment for anything is not justice, but vengeance, cruelty, and hate. I tell you straight, this just God of yours is nothing but the reflection of your own dirty mind, which is still back in the days when they hanged a woman for stealing ribbon. You may twist yourself into philosophic knots as much as you like, and pile up explanations that don't explain to your heart's content, but you cannot get over the fact that a "justice" which demanded everlasting punishment for anything would be just another name for inhuman brutality. That is all this divine "justice" is, it is a survival, a superstition in the worst sense.

'What I want to know is, Why did Jesus suffer? What good did His sufferings do? What difference do they make to-day? What good purpose was served by them which could not have been served without? If you cannot give me intelligible answers of some sort, I am prepared to pity Jesus, as I am prepared to pity any other noble visionary who has been put to death, because he was before his time, but I do not see why I should worship Him because of His sufferings, which are just one more gruesome act in this world's sordid tragedy of errors. I admire the men who suffered for me in the war, because I see what good their sufferings did, I see what they have saved me from, and I don't see how I could have been saved without them. But I cannot see what good the sufferings of Jesus did, or what they have saved me from, or why, if there be an Almighty God of Love, I could not have been saved without them. I cannot see why men should not have been forgiven, if they repented, without this brutal murder as a sacrifice. Jesus forgave men freely when He was on earth, and never Himself mentioned any other condition of forgiveness but repentance. He told us to forgive seventy times seven if a man repents, and went further, and told us to forgive our enemies, bless those who cursed us, and do good to those who ill-treated us, and that we were to do this because we have to be perfect as our Father in Heaven is perfect. Yet you say that a callous legal murder had to be committed before it was possible for God to forgive a repentant man. To be quite frank, this doctrine strikes me as being not merely incredible, but immoral as well.

> "Blest through endless ages
> Be the precious stream
> Which from endless torments
> Did the world redeem"

is bad morality put into poor poetry, and sung to a sorry tune.'

These questions, half formulated, and altogether unexpressed, crowd into the mind of the man and woman in the street when he or she is persuaded to come and be saved, and the preacher pleads pathetically for gratitude to Christ for His bitter sufferings. Visions of similar brutalities which he has seen and is anxious to forget flit before the soldier's mind - men with their bowels in their hands, men with bodies ripped and torn, murdered children, ravished women; and the great God who needed a propitiation to save the world from sin, and then did not save it, sits up and looks down on it all. The preacher cannot explain. The theologian explains himself into a knot which no one could untie. Dr. Dale explained the Atonement to me as a youth, and was harder to grasp than the Cross itself. Dr. Moberly was worse. I have never read a book on the Atonement that did not puzzle me more than the puzzle. As for getting a plain message for plain men out of them, it would take God Himself to do it, no man could. The miracle was that God sometimes did. He can get through any cloud of lies to find a soul in desperate need.

Plain men do not understand justice that demands eternal punishment, and cannot picture a Father who requires propitiation before He forgives a repentant child. The fact is that our preachers spend, or did spend (they have largely given it up as a bad job now and taken to brief, bright, and brotherly talks to the people on popular subjects, with sacred solos by Miss Jinks), their time explaining, not the Gospel, but the symbols and metaphors which its first evangelists used in the struggle to give its message to the men of their day, men whose minds moved in a different world from ours, men whose religion was steeped in bloody sacrifice, whose states, were ruled by despots, and whose work was done by slaves, men whose idea of justice was full of cruelty and destitute of love. We sacrifice reason and imperil morality in order to keep these pseudo-sacred symbols and metaphors intact. It all leaves the decent man in the street cold. He finds it dull, dreary, and repulsive. Better go out into God's green fields and listen to the choir of birds, better to see God's Love in a cloudless sky, than sit in a stuffy church and hear a perspiring parson wrestling to explain how 'Justice' and the awful Holiness of God demanded a peculiarly brutal murder as propitiation in order to avoid damning a world of men to Hell.

They have my sympathy. But there is a sublimely simple truth that saves. Get all that out of your head. Burn all the books of explanation.

Fisherise the whole boiling and sack the lot. ('This is dreadful,' exclaims the nice good man who thinks such things too sacred to talk naturally about. 'What becomes of Catholic theology?' I don't know - and - Oh, I don't want to be contemptuous or anything, but I don't care. As a matter of fact, I have never been able to discover what Catholic theology is. It changes with every generation of Catholics. It cometh up, and is cut down like a flower, and never continueth in one stay. It is the mortal body of an immortal truth. Which is the Catholic religion.) We have suffered many things for these dead symbols, it is time that some one read their funeral service, and they were decently interred in a museum. Let us get out. Swing back to the universe as it is. Here we stand beneath the stars, with the challenge of the world before us. What does it mean?

Remember what we know. Remember first that it is a movement - an unfinished movement. It is on a pilgrimage - a journey. Where to? That is the question. And it is in order to answer that question, and only to answer that question, 'Where to?' that we have turned back and asked ourselves the question, 'Where from?' We have sought to pierce the darkness of the past in the hope of discerning the direction in which the world is moving, and so guessing the final goal to which it strives. We have seen the agelong preparation of the world for life, and then the strange beginnings of life itself. We have traced its struggle upwards stage by stage, we have seen vegetable, animal, human life emerge, and we have marked how each higher type of life has had to struggle for its existence, only surviving if it proved strong enough to overcome the lower life. That has been true in the story of man as in the story of animals and things. We have watched the growth of man, and have gained the impression that behind and within it there seems to be a Power which makes for unity of man with man, which strives to make the Human Unity or Brotherhood, to create Man. We have marked the growth of unity against the obstacles of human stupidity, imperfection, and sin, and in that growth there came a crisis, a break through, parallel partly with those great crises when life itself began, or when mind emerged out of matter, there came the crisis of Christmas Day - the Incarnation. In the fullness of time God broke through once more, and a higher life than the merely human, a new order of goodness, appeared upon earth, and appeared as a solitary Personality amid millions of a lower order of life. What would you expect, what would the whole story of the process lead you to expect? Are not Gethsemane and Calvary, or something like them, natural, inevitable? Was it not written in the rocks and stones, written in the strange book of Life's history, that the Son of Man must suffer many things, and be rejected of the elders and chief priests and scribes - the whole of the lower and older order of life; and was it not written, too, that He must be raised up - that the higher order must survive? Can you not almost see that naked Figure, with His wonder and His wounds, growing out of the pages of your scientific textbook? Has not the whole process been the crucifixion of the higher by the lower life, is it not all summed up in the Cross? The process is bloody, so is the Cross; the process is repulsive, so is the Cross; the process is unjust, so is the Cross; the process is glorious, so is the Christ. Behold the Man - Perfect Man - the Character. Never does His glory shine so brightly as it shines now. No man has ever seen the sun who has not seen it break its way through inky clouds and bathe the world in sudden silver beauty from on high, so no man ever sees the Face of God until it breaks upon his vision through the clouds of Calvary. Never was God so human, never was man so Divine.

"Tis that weakness in strength that I cry for - my flesh that I seek
    In the Godhead. I seek it and find it. O man, it shall be
    A face like my face that receives thee, a Man like to me
Thou shalt love and be loved by for ever; a hand like this hand
Shall open the gates of New Life to thee - See the Christ stand.'

This is the truth: the martyrdom of God in Man, not the punishment of Man by God.

This is the truth that lies behind all these old-world symbols and metaphors, behind the Propitiation and the Sacrifice. The Incarnation is the Atonement - and the Atonement the Incarnation. Good Friday is Christmas Day, and Christmas Day Good Friday, and Easter Day, and Ascension Day, and Whitsunday, because they are all Christ. It is Christ that saves, not the Cross; it is Christ that redeems, not His sufferings. The Cross does not save, any more than the process creates. The Cross never saved any man, and never could. You are not to be saved by anything that happened in the past, you can only be saved by God acting now in the present. You cannot be saved by any Church, Sacrament, Priest, or Creed of God - you can only be saved by God Himself. Calvary is not past, it is present. The Cross is still set up, the crowd still stands and mocks, the soldiers still play dice, the faithful still draw near to worship God in Man. That Christ Who hung there hangs there still, and calls to you and me, challenging us to take up the struggle of the higher life, bear its burden, endure its shame, and win its inward Peace.

The Cross was the most natural thing in the world - the most natural and inevitable, as natural and as inevitable as all the rest of the hideous process by which life has been, and is being, evolved, and of which it is the first scene in the final act. There is no Almighty potentate who made the world perfect, and then permitted it to come to a disaster, put it under a curse for thousands of years, and then intervened and sent His Son to undo the curse by offering a propitiatory sacrifice. It is all a tissue of ancient metaphors in which men strive to express in terms of their day the overwhelming experience of finding God in Christ. He had to be expressed in terms of their religion and their philosophy, but we are not bound by them, or saved by believing in them. We are only bound by the Spirit of Christ, saved by our faith in Him, not in what He was, nor in what He did, but in what He is, and has been from the beginning, from the time that this mysterious business first began and the world of worlds was born. The Gospel does not ask men to believe in suffering as being good, or as being the Will of God. The Cross was no more the Will of God than any other murder or atrocity that stains the story of man's life on earth. The Cross is common, it is Christ that is unique. It was no more the Will of God that Christ should suffer than it is the Will of God that a good and patient wife should have her brains battered out by a drunken husband with the leg of a table, or that a young mother should be ripped open and left disembowelled on her own doorstep by a drunken soldier. It was the Will of God that the travail of the process should bring in the fullness of time the perfect Life to birth, and that it should be lived out in its perfection to the end. It was God's Will, because God was and is that Life, and He was travailing in the process, and is travailing still.

The necessity of Calvary was the necessity that has been binding on God since the beginning of time, it was the necessity inherent in the task of creation. We can never fully understand it, any more than we can fully understand anything else. It is not sufficient to account for the facts to say that God chose to give man a free will, and that man chose evil rather than good. There is a truth in that, but it is not, cannot be, the whole truth. All the misery and evil in the world, all the cruelty and crime, is not due now, and never has been due, to man's deliberate choice of evil. It was not merely sin - in the full sense of wilful sin - that has caused God's agelong Calvary, or that hung Christ on the Cross. All through the ages men have crucified God, not knowing what they did, crucified Him through their ignorance, stupidity, and imperfection as well as through deliberate choice of wrong against right. There has always been a voice crying in the heart of God, and appealing to His Fatherhood, 'Forgive them, for they know not what they do.' It is not possible to account for all the hideous misery that has marked the growth of Man as being the consequence of sin - unless you interpret sin in a wider sense than the word can really bear. It must be taken to include ignorance, dullness of imagination, feebleness of mind, and a host of other factors for which man cannot be held wholly responsible either as an individual or as a race. Religion in the past has suffered because it concentrated all its attention on sin' as deliberate rebellion against God, and passed over the part that ignorance and feebleness have played in making His agelong Calvary. This has been due to the fact that we have separated the Creation of the world from its Redemption, basing our thought upon the doctrine of the Fall and man's free will. But there is a sense in which Creation and Redemption go on side by side, and have always gone on side by side, because the Creator and Redeemer are One God. Redemption is not an afterthought of the Creator - it is an eternal aspect of His work. The Lamb was slain from the foundation of the world. There has always been a Calvary in God's heart.

The first and last enemy of God the Creator, is Death - nothingness, non-existence. That is what evil is in its essence - nothingness. Evil is self-destructive and tends to death; it is based on a lie and ends nowhere. God's first creative act brought Him up against the enemy, and He has been up against it ever since, and must be up against it until creation is complete, and the world is made at last.

Calvary is the revelation in human terms of what Creation - Creation in that larger, truer sense which includes Redemption - means to God. It is the struggle of Life with Death. Christ is Life and the Cross is Death. Man is saved by Life and not by Death, by Christ and not by the Cross. When we say that man has free will, we mean that he has become conscious of the struggle of Life with Death in the world and in himself, and can resolve or refuse to co-operate with Life. Sin, deliberate sin, is conscious refusal to accept the struggle for existence which Life must make - conscious refusal to bear the Cross. The only cure for sin is Life - more Life. The selfish man is a dying man. His world is small and must grow smaller. The loving man is a living man. His world is large, and must grow larger. What the world needs, what it always has needed, is more Life. That is what Christ can and does give, not by what He did, nor by what He was, but by what He does, and by what He is now - the same yesterday, to-day, and for ever. God does not punish the sinner; sin is its own punishment; it means inevitable decay, and decay is painful, and it ends in death - extinction. The pain may not be terrible, may not be anything like as keen as the pain of growth, but it is useless and ends nowhere.

Now we have cleared some clouds away, and the Christ stands out from His Cross, and in Him is Life Eternal. When you accept the challenge to follow Him, you do not promise to model your thoughts, words, and actions upon the pattern of One Who was alive and is dead, but to surrender in utter loyalty to One Who was dead and is alive again and for ever. It is not by the sufferings of Christ that you are saved, but by His Life-force; it is not the Cross you are called upon to worship, but the Christ, Who is the Life of the World.

IX.   *Dead and Buried*

YOU cannot expect a Christian-and by a Christian I mean a person who has set out honestly and with determined purpose to seek for himself and for his fellow-men the Jesus order of goodness, that new and Eternal. Life which came to earth in Christ - I say you cannot expect a Christian to talk or write about the Death of Jesus Christ upon the Cross without very deep feeling. I doubt if it ought to be possible for anybody, any fully human being, to contemplate that Death without some feeling. No tragedy that dramatic genius has ever staged is half so poignant and so piercing in its pathos as the simple Passion story of St. Matthew or St. Luke.

If, as some of the scholars seem to think, the Passion of Jesus is a legend based upon some ancient mystery play, then the author of that mystery play was a genius who knocked Shakespeare into a cocked hat. The greatest artists and the greatest musicians have felt their highest powers fail to do the slightest justice to the Gospel Story. Bach halts and Handel falters as they draw near the end. All the sorrows and all the glories of human history surround and are summed up in Calvary. Stand alone on that little hill, and you can hear the weeping and the songs of triumph of countless worlds of men and women who have journeyed out of the darkness into the light and out into the darkness again. The heart of humanity turns thither in its bitterest hours, and feels a friend draw near. Explanations seem futile, criticism becomes impertinent and absurd. Let it stand alone, that Central Cross, and tell its own heart-piercing tale. Words can only serve to veil its glory and dim the radiance of its beauty for the suffering soul of man.

This is no place for asking questions or weaving theological theories. Go down upon your knees. This is the central mystery of the Christian Faith -

'There was no other good enough
To pay the price of sin;
He only could unlock the gate
Of Heaven, and let us in.'

That is all you need. Let the pathos of the Cross have its way and break the hearts of men with its tremendous appeal, 'This have I done for thee; what wilt thou do for Me?' That is the instinct of the Christian. It is natural, and in some ways it is supremely right, but in other ways it is wrong and extremely dangerous; it leads to a religion of feeling divorced from thought, a religion that is pathetic but not powerful, and that is no good. A religion which is without feeling is a poor thing, but a religion which is all feeling is not religious at all, it is only sentimental. The last thing in the world that Christ was or wanted to be was pathetic. He was no writer of tragedies, He was a Saviour of men. He was the most practical person that ever lived. The last thing He wanted to do was to set souls sailing on a sea of tears to nowhere in particular. Emotions are like shadows passing over cornfields; they come and go, and come again, and leave no trace behind. Christ wants more than our tears, He wants our very selves, the very fibre of our beings yielded up to Him. He either wants you to go the whole hog or not to go at all: you cannot put Him off with the easy tribute that you pay to Sidney Carton on the stage. This is not drama, it is reality, and we have got to ask questions, and we have got to demand answers; we cannot be put off by false reverence or talk of mystery. God's mysteries were meant to lead us on to their solution, not to bar us out from hope of truth. The Cross is a challenge. What does it mean? What did He do for men? What did He save them from? How did He save them? Why did His death save them? What do you mean by being washed in the blood of the Lamb?

We have got to ask these questions, we have got to seek an answer. Men have always asked them and always sought for answers, and there has never been a satisfying one yet. It is no good trying to pretend that there has been one consistent Christian answer, because there never has been. If you doubt that, get hold of any review[1] you like of the writings of the Christian Fathers about the meaning of the Cross, from St. Paul to Dr. Dale, and if your head does not whirl with the multitude of theories, I am prepared to eat my Sunday hat.

There you see the spectacle of men - good and holy men, and very brainy men too - wrestling to express what the Life and Death of Jesus meant to them, in terms of their knowledge and their thought, and you get up with a sigh, muttering to yourself, 'Good Lord, what a business this Christianity is!' And yet, it is perfectly evident that behind all these weird and wonderful theories there is a tremendous and shattering experience which these men are out to express, an experience of Salvation which is all bound up with Calvary. It is perfectly evident that behind the chaos of Christian theology there burns the unquenchable fire of the Christian religion. It is impossible to make a seamless robe out of the patchwork quilt of Christian theology, impossible to make a consistent whole out of this multitude of conflicting theories. Yet they all have some common features: they all start and are based upon the doctrine of the Fall of Man.

All alike start from that great day when God the Supreme Creator King looked down upon His world, His finished and completed world, and saw that it was good. Every stone was in its place, every star stood to its course, no discord broke the harmony that God had wrought, as day by day the sun went down and the moon rose up to bathe God's garden in

---

[1]   Dr. Rashdall's *Idea of the Atonement in Christian Theology* would be as good a Review as any.

the silver of its peace. There in that garden, innocent, sinless, naked, and unashamed, man walked with his own mate and talked with God his friend as the evening shadows fell. Then on a sudden, from somewhere, from somewhere outside the picture, there comes a jarring note, a discord. Evil comes into the world, and Paradise is lost. There is no hint of where it comes from, save that it is said to be an echo of a discord that arose in Heaven itself among the angels that surrounded the Throne of God. Man innocent, but perfectly free to choose between right and wrong, chooses wrong; then a cloud comes over the earth and hides the Face of God, the world falls under a curse, man becomes a rebel, and the justice of the great offended God demands that he should be punished for his rebellion.

Years pass by, and then there comes a sudden and tremendous intervention on the part of the angry and offended God, and all the world is drowned except a few choice souls that are left floating on the waters in the Ark of the Lord. But even that drastic punishment does not stay the disease. The curse of sin continues and eats its way into the soul of man. The whole of the race is doomed, for the justice of God demands that the soul that sins should die. But God conceives a wonderful scheme to repair the disaster and save mankind from the awful doom of death and eternal pain that, apart from the scheme, inevitably awaits them. Of all the nations in the world He chooses one, and by a long course of education and of chastisement He prepares them for the coming of His Son, the Saviour of mankind. He gives them a divinely inspired code of laws, and orders, religious rites, and ceremonies to be performed, all of which in various ways look forward to and foreshadow the coming of the Christ. From time to time He sends them prophets who plead with and recall them to the service of the one true God against Whom they consciously and knowingly rebelled. And then at last the great day dawns, and the Saviour comes, and every detail of His Life and Death is worked out in accordance with the Divine foreshadowing and the Divine plan. In accordance with that plan Christ moves on His appointed way from Bethlehem to Calvary, and on the Cross reveals the meaning of the Temple Altars running red with the blood of sacrifice, and of all the rites and ceremonies that God had fore-ordained.

He is the Great Sacrifice and Propitiation, and by His Death upon the Cross He takes away the curse, satisfies the justice of God, saves us from His wrath, and opens out the way of Salvation. His Death upon the Cross was the climax of God's plan, it was the great necessity. By that death He removed the curse, by becoming 'a curse' for us. So the Death of Christ becomes the centre of the Christian Gospel, and faith in the power of that Death to save us becomes the only means of Salvation. Christ's Death upon the Cross was the only propitiation that was, or could be, offered to turn away the just wrath of God from sinful man. To whom the Sacrifice and Propitiation was offered has always been vague. Some said it was to the Devil, some said it was made to the Father, some said it was made by the love of the Father to the Father's justice, but the Church has never been certain to whom it was made.

That is a fairly just, though superficial, sketch of the 'common element' in the many answers that have been given to the great questions of how, and why, and from what Christ saves us. But the worst of it is that we cannot take this common element and make it our own, because it is just this very scheme of Salvation, just this very Divine plan, which has become utterly incredible to us. It is not that it has been proved untrue, it is that it has become unreal. It has not been murdered, it has died a natural death, it has ceased to grip. It has around it always the atmosphere of a fairy tale; inwardly we feel that it is impossible, it lies right outside the circle of our thought. You see, it starts off by contradicting at the very beginning our whole idea of the universe. We cannot believe in that great day when God looked down upon His completed world and saw that it was good, because the world never was completed, and is not completed yet. The universe to us is an uncompleted growth, with God as its Life-force. We find it impossible to believe that man has ever been as God meant him to be and then fallen from that, because all our knowledge of the history of man leads us to believe that he has grown up stage by stage from the animal, and never has been as God meant him to be, and is not yet. We cannot believe in this perfectly peaceful garden world, in which there was no struggle, no bitterness or strife, when everything tends to tell us that nature has always been as she is now, red in tooth and claw, ruthless and cruel, and that man, like every other creature, has had to struggle for his existence. We find no place in this picture for that tremendous struggle which man, like the beasts, has had to face with bleeding hands and a breaking heart all down the years.

The background of the world's beginning, our new Book of Genesis, is the story of a fierce and terrible struggle between beast and beast and man and man, which it is impossible for us to regard as having been due to the anger of God for sin, because it seems to be the very tissue of nature itself, and began before there was any sin to be angry about. The new Adam that science draws for us is not a being whom we could regard as in any sense complete or satisfactory to God. Even in his earliest days he must have been fighting, fierce and ruthless in his cunning, or he would never have survived. He must have been a very different creature from that peaceful Adam of the garden to whom the beasts were friends. Nevertheless, the fact that the legend of the golden age of happiness in the dim past of man is a world-wide legend, found in the folklore of almost every people on the earth, shows that it must have some truth behind it, and we can believe that there was a time when man was very little above the animal, and was hardly self-conscious at all; when he fitted his environment as the animals fit theirs, and was not yet troubled with the dreams, the aspirations, and the everlasting discontent which are the hall-mark of humanity as we know it. We can believe in a time which was in truth the childhood of the race, and which has become, as our own childhood always does become, a thing o£. beauty which grows more beautiful and more rainbow-coloured as it fades into the past.

What we cannot believe is that it was really as pure and bright and peaceful as it has been depicted from the distance of after years, or that all the sorrow and cruelty of history - its wars, oppressions, tyrannies, and tortures - have been due to the fact that the first man wilfully and deliberately rejected God. We cannot believe that but for that first sin the progress of man would have been an orderly and painless advance to perfection. History - the history of man - is too painfully parallel with the struggle among the beasts for us to believe that all its chaos was due to wilful rebellion. Partly it must always have been due, as it is now, to man's imperfection, his ignorance of truth, for which he is only partly responsible. The chaos of human history, like the chaos of a human nursery, is partly due to sin, and partly to childish ignorance for which neither the children nor their parents are wholly to blame.

Looked at in this light, the whole vision of God is different. We no longer sit in a law court and listen to a great judge proclaiming a sentence of just doom upon a sinful man; we see rather a great Poet wrestling to express Himself in His poem, with all the mingled joy and sorrow, the success through constant failure, of the creative mind at work; we see rather a great Father striving to create perfect sons, and suffering always for their ignorance and sin; we see a great Life-force breaking through into a new form of life, and suffering agonies to give that new form of life permanence and strength. Nor does this vision of God, as is commonly supposed, lessen or do away with the sinfulness of sin. We cannot believe that man was ever perfectly free or perfectly responsible for the wrongs he did. The sorrow and suffering cannot indeed be wholly due to wilful sin; partly they are, and always must have been, the result, not of man's wilful rebellion, but of man's ignorance and imperfection - his childishness. Nevertheless, we can and must believe that from the very beginning, ever since man was man in any real sense, he has had a certain measure of freedom and a certain measure of responsibility, and that he has misused that, and has laid upon the great creative Spirit the double agony of Creation and Redemption, the double task of enlightening his ignorance and turning him from his sin, and these two tasks have been going on side by side, this double burden has been borne by God, ever since man was man, and so the Lamb was slain from the foundation of the world. There has always been a Crucifix in Heaven's heart of hearts.

With this new vision of man's genesis there comes a new vision of the Cross. The vision of the judge and His awful justice, and of that impending and appalling doom, vanishes from Calvary as it does from the Garden of Eden. We no longer feel bound to the metaphors and symbols that are based upon the old Book of Genesis. If we cling to the great words, Sacrifice and Propitiation, we give to them an entirely new meaning; we think of them in terms of life and not of death. We find ourselves, as we ought to find ourselves, utterly unable to think of or contemplate the Cross apart from the Empty Tomb, and Christ's Death apart from His Resurrection. It is not that He died, but that He rose again; it is not the Death, but the Life, the unconquerable and insuperable Life, that becomes to us the important point.

In the light of the doctrine of development the meaning of the Cross shines out more brightly, with fiercer and more burning power than it could ever do against the background of the Fall, the judge, and the awful doom. The old words take on new meanings. He is the New Life, the supreme and perfect manifestation of God, the great Life-force, the Eternal Life doing battle with death and overcoming it. He is our Sacrifice and Propitiation in the Spirit, because the idea of a Sacrifice was the giving of something up to God with which you identified yourself, and which was the offering of yourself to Him. Christ, the Living Christ, is our sacrifice, because it is the Christ living in us, the Christ Spirit born in our hearts, that we offer up to God as the only ground, and the only possible ground, of our communion with Him. It is Christ crucified in us, the new form of Life struggling for its existence in us, that is our only hope of perfection. Only as we become partakers of that Life can we hope for perfection.

That is just bed-rock truth. Looked at in the highest light, looked at as God must look at me, there is nothing in the ordinary me, nothing in myself, that is worth anything, it is only this Spirit of self-sacrificing love, this Spirit of purity and supreme nobility, that makes me worth anything at all, or makes any man worth anything at all. He is our propitiation, because, once more, a propitiation is something that you offer up to God instead of yourself, and it is the ever-dying yet deathless Christ in my heart that I offer up to God instead of myself. It is not any act of His that I offer up, it is not anything that He did in the past, it is Him Himself, alive in me, Christ in me, the Hope of Glory. He is my propitiation.

The great thing that Jesus did for us was not to die but to live, and His Death is only valued as a witness to his Deathlessness; the Atonement is the climax of the Incarnation; they are not two, but one truth.

The great glory of the new idea, the idea of movement, progress, and development, the great light that it sheds upon the Cross, is that it fixes our eyes and our hopes, not upon the Death, but upon the Life of Christ, and upon His Death only as the vindication of His Deathlessness.

Thus the Birth, Death, and Resurrection of Christ are seen to be one truth, one revelation of what God is like. We get rid at one stroke of the fairy-tale atmosphere. We no longer have the judge proclaiming the awful doom upon the whole race, cursing the earth and sending disease, pestilence, and famine as punishment for man's sin, and holding over them the threat of still more awful punishment to come, a vision of God which is torture to our highest moral instincts. We no longer have the vision of a supremely Almighty Being Who creates a perfect world, and then permits it to go wrong and fails to put it right by the most drastic punishment, and fails likewise to put it right by His wonderful scheme of Salvation. We are no longer walking in the pious twilight of outworn traditions, we come out into the sunlight of fact and of things we know. We do know that there has been a Life-force from the very beginning continuously expressing itself in higher and higher forms of life. We do know that each higher form of life has had to struggle for its existence; we do see in the Life of Jesus and His Character the highest form of life that ever appeared upon this planet. We would naturally expect that that higher form of life would have to struggle and strive for its existence. Everything that we know of the world would lead us to expect Calvary. It was prophesied not merely by the Hebrew prophets, but by all the million voices of prophecy which have been since the world began. And everything we know of the world would lead us to expect Easter Day, lead us to expect that the great Life-force which, through failure, has so often triumphed would, through failure, triumph once again.

And now to me the whole thing becomes simple; I know where I am. To begin with, I know what God is like, He is revealed to me in the Life of Jesus. God, Who commanded the light to shine out of the darkness, has shined into my heart to give the light of the knowledge of the Glory of God *in the Face of Jesus Christ,* and that is my greatest need satisfied; I know Him in Whom I have believed. There is no Great Unknown, no Veiled Being, to Whose inscrutable judgments I must perforce submit, even when they violate my sense of right and wrong.

God is like Jesus. I know what I mean when I ask God to forgive me 'for Jesus Christ's sake.' I have got no sort of idea in my mind about the awful, far-off, dreadfully Holy judge who spares me eternal punishment because of a ghastly sacrifice over two thousand years ago. I have the vision of the great creative Father with Whom I seek to be at one, and I know that the only possible reason I have for expecting that I can be at one with Him is that there is in me something of the Spirit of Jesus, something of His Divinely perfect humanity. It is not mine, and it is not me, it is a gift from God, a gift which comes to me through His Cross, and through His Saints, through His martyrs, and His Church. The New Life is in me, the Life of Jesus Christ, and because of Him, alive though crucified, in me, I can seek and find forgiveness with God. I know what I mean when I say that I am 'washed in the Blood of the Lamb,' for blood is Life, Life given and outpoured, and it is by the outpouring of the New Life into me that I am saved. It is not merely because He was crucified once and rose again two thousand years ago, but because by that act He is revealed as crucified, yet always rising again in me, that I am being saved, and that I hope at last to be completely saved. I know also what I am saved from; not from any curse of God (an impossible conception), not from any eternal punishment for sin in the world to come, but from sin itself, from selfishness, from meanness, from greed, from the sin which is its own hell. Thus I find the very heart of the Christian Faith and cast away its husk. God is revealed to me in Christ, and I can know Him as He is, and in that growing knowledge find Eternal Life. The only trouble that I have left is that the shadow of those old beliefs, those ancient fears, the shadow of the awful judge and of His dreadful justice, lies over the liturgies and forms of service that I am obliged to use; the atmosphere of the fairy tale still is within the Church, and I have to spend so much of my time explaining that the words of the Prayer Book do not mean what they say, but something different, and it all seems to be such waste of time. And yet I know that the new meaning does beat through the old words, that the new truth does find expression in the old symbols. I believe that it always has found expression through them, and that so far as Christ has saved men, He has always saved them by the power of the revelation of Himself and of God's love in the Cross. The religion has always been right, and men have never been able to make it of no effect through their traditions. But the time has now come when we should lift from our people the load of misunderstanding that arises from our tangle of outworn metaphors.

The whole of this bewildering cycle of theories of the Atonement arises from the attempt to reconcile two irreconcilable visions of God, the attempt to keep the God of the Old Testament and worship the God of the New. From the time of St. Paul onwards this attempt has broken the brains and the hearts of men. The time has now come when we can be set free from that burden altogether, and throw ourselves completely upon the God revealed in Christ.

'Bread of Thy Body give me for my fighting,
Give me to drink of Thy sacred Blood for wine,
While there are wrongs that need me for the righting,
While there is warfare, splendid and Divine.

'Give me for light the sunshine of Thy sorrow,
Give me for shelter the shadow of Thy Cross,
Bid me to share the Glory of to-morrow,
And gone from my heart is the bitterness of loss.'

X. He descended into Hell

I HAVE met a good few honest men and women who are out for reality in religion, who have said to me that if the two statements, 'Born of the Virgin Mary' and 'He descended into Hell' could be omitted, the short Creed of Christendom would be to them a complete and inspiring symbol of the great unseen reality for which their spirits crave; but these two statements bother them, and on the whole they would rather have left them out. Not so much because they felt they were untrue as because they felt they were unreal and unneeded, they did not add anything to them. I can understand that, but I do not think it will do. We have seen how great and clear a challenge to the world is involved in the doctrine of the Virgin Birth; we have seen that that picture of the Holy Family - the spotless Mother, the strong, protective Father, and the Holy Child - is, as it were, the big drum of Christendom, beating out its summons to the life of purity and its challenge to the battle with the flesh; and behind this other clause, the descent into Hell, there lies a challenge too. In this again Christ's trumpet calls us to the parting of the ways. Here for the first time the Creed swings out into another world; death is not the end, it says, there is more to come. Life is more than a matter of life and death, it is a matter of life and death - and the Beyond. Good and evil, truth and falsehood are not mere matters of welfare and happiness in this world, their effects and consequences reach out into another sphere. The Creed calls us to bet our lives upon the fact that five minutes after death we shall be conscious, thinking, feeling, knowing, sorrowing, and joying. It calls us to believe that there is another sphere of life which lies so close to this that within three minutes from now I could be there if I would. It only needs a revolver or some prussic acid, and I could be there in three minutes from now. It is now three o'clock; at three minutes past three I could, if I would, be standing in that other land. It is nearer to me than London is, in fact it is nearer than Mrs. Hunt's tobacco shop just round the corner.

Perhaps it is partly because of the words in which it is expressed that the challenge is not so much realised. Hell is a word which has gathered around it a strange and awful association of ideas: it stands for a doctrine which thousands of thinking, loving people hate with all their hearts, the doctrine of eternal punishment; and even though we know quite well that it is not in this sense that the word is used here, the association of ideas clings around it still, and plays a very large part in turning men away from thought about the real truth this statement of the Creed is put there to express. If we could say instead of 'He descended into Hell,' 'and so passed on to Paradise,' if we could say, 'I believe in Jesus Christ His Only Son our Lord, Who was conceived by the Holy Ghost, born of the Virgin

Mary, suffered under Pontius Pilate, was crucified, dead, and buried, and so passed on to Paradise,' I think the meaning of the challenge would grow clearer; it would also link the clause on with Christ's own words upon the Cross, 'To-day thou shalt be with Me in Paradise.' The Creed calls us to believe that what He Himself said would happen did actually happen, and that His Spirit went forth to meet that of the friendly and repentant thief in another world, and that as His Spirit passed, so, when death knocks at our doors, shall we pass too. It does not call us as yet to the belief in immortality, only to belief in survival, only to the belief that death is not final. Immortality and survival are two entirely different things. It does not prove that because my personality survives death it is therefore immortal. It is well to remember that, because great numbers of us are prone to mistake what is merely evidence for survival as being evidence of immortality. Even if the fact of the possibility of communication between ourselves and departed spirits were proved up to the hilt, beyond all possibility of dispute, it would not prove that the soul was immortal, but merely that it survived the ordeal of death. And the Christian Creed does not ask us to believe in the least that survival has in itself anything to do with the Life or Death of Christ. Quite apart from Christ, the human soul survives death and lives in another world, a world in which its fate depends upon its use of its life here.

It is a strange, and to many sore hearts rather a baffling and bewildering thing, that Christ tells us so little about the world beyond, almost nothing definite or explicit. Many books have been written trying to gather up into a clear and consistent picture all the hints He leaves us, but most of them are pious guess-work, and they are not convincing. A great deal has been made of the parable of Dives and Lazarus, but it does not really bear the weight that has been placed upon it. The purpose of the story seems to be not so much to give us information about the nature of the life beyond, which is described altogether in the terms of the Jewish thought of Christ's day, as to drive home those lessons about the after life which went through the whole of Christ's teaching about it. The lessons are few and simple. There is another life. Our fate there depends upon our conduct here. The great misuse of this life, which reaps inevitable sorrow in that, is selfishness, the use of life for the service of self. The rich man in the parable is the typical selfish man, who works out in the after world the inevitable consequence of his selfishness, which is separation from God, the Spirit of Love. Beyond that, I do not think there is much that we can learn from the parable without forcing it. The whole purpose of it is moral and ethical. Christ does not seem to be supplying information to clairvoyants so much as giving a solemn warning to profiteers.

Exactly the same can be said of the Great judgment picture in St. Matthew, where the sheep are parted from the goats. The main purpose of the picture is a moral purpose, it sets out to teach in vivid and compelling terms the truth that good and evil, love and selfishness have consequences that reach out beyond this world and continue after death.

No man or nation here can come to the Father, no man or nation here can fulfil their destiny and calling, except by Him, that is, unless they seriously set out to win for themselves the Jesus order of goodness. The acceptance or rejection of Love as it is revealed in Christ is a choice the final results of which lie away and beyond our joy and sorrow in this life. The great purpose of the picture does not seem to be the rending of the veil that hides the future from us and the disclosing in detail of what is yet to come; the surroundings of that Second Advent, the Throne, the Angels, and the Glory, are once more the conventional surroundings of Christ's time, taken from the apocalyptic writings of the day. The whole point seems to be that the judgment is going to be a moral judgment; it is going to be a question of character, a matter of whether we accept or reject Love as revealed in Christ, and that the acceptance of Love means a new and wonderful bliss which is not of this world, while its rejection leads inevitably to a new and awful sorrow which is not of this world either.

If we confine ourselves to what Christ actually taught, that seems to be the sum total of it. Nowhere does He satisfy our natural curiosity, nowhere does He reveal to us details of what we may expect; it is always the same great lesson of tremendous hope and awful warning. There, as here, He is to be the judge, because there, as here, He is the everlasting Lover of mankind; there, as here, the Character is to stand and point with a loving but relentless finger to the sins that stain our souls.

To those who have lost their best beloved, and have watched the passing of the spirit out through the gate of death, or who have not had even that comfort, and do not even know where the bodies of their dead are lying, the New Testament is, in the first flush of their sorrow, a disappointing book. A thousand and one things that they would love to know are not revealed; a thousand and one questions that they would ask of Christ He leaves unanswered. He has very little more to say in answer to the great question, What next? than what could be summed up in four words, 'More Life with Me,' and that is all, unless we add to it the awful possibility, 'More life without Me,' and so put before ourselves, as He for ever put before men and women, the great choice.

That is all Christ has to say, and although it is disappointing to those whose torn hearts crave for details, it is in itself enough to challenge the whole thought of the world that strives to live without God. It is a challenge to the ordinary worldly morality. There are thousands of men in the world to-day who care nothing for Christ and nothing for God, who are quite prepared to patronise and support the Church because they believe it is good for society. It tends to make people respectable and law-abiding, it makes them more contented and submissive to things as they are. These people are quite prepared to invest large sums of money in religion as an insurance against rebellion and unrest, while they never give a thought to the life beyond, have not a shadow of belief that the consequences of what they do or leave undone can have any effect upon a world beyond this one. Some of them accept as a matter of course the ordinary belief in a vague kind of Heaven, but it does not affect their lives. They give their money to feed the poor, but have not love, and so they are worth nothing in Christ's eyes, they are still in the dark. However respectable and respected they may be, however much they preside at public meetings for good objects, and however much their subscriptions may be to hospitals and institutions for the prevention of vice, their eyes are still blind to the great light, their minds still move within the narrow confines of a life that ends with death, they have not seen the truth, they have not perceived the real nature of good and evil, they do not know the difference between righteousness and expediency; life is still to them a matter of profit and loss in this world.

There are thousands more men who would not support the Church or any form of Christianity, who believe that the questions of right and wrong are to be judged solely from the point of view of this world, on the principle of the greatest happiness for the greatest number. Frankly, they worship comfort instead of Christ. Their idea of man is not the striving, struggling, aspiring soul with the everlasting ideal still shining before him, but a sleek, fat, well-fed, well-housed, and completely satisfied individual, who sleeps and eats and loves and laughs in perfect and complete content. This idea lies at the bottom of the baser sort of Socialism, which seeks a way out of our social cares by a road downhill toward the beast.

Against both of these, against the Lord Mayor with the white whiskers who invests money in Christianity as an insurance policy against labour troubles, and against the social reformer who strives for a comfortable and Godless world, the teaching of Christ proclaims war and cries, 'Thou fool, this night shall thy soul be required of thee.' There is another world, and more and more as the clouds clear away from the arena of battle, and we see where we are, it will be found that the struggle of the future lies between those who believe that the soul passes on to Paradise and those who do not believe that there is a soul to pass or a Paradise to pass to.

This is true, and this challenge is contained in the clause, 'He descended into Hell.' Do you believe that five minutes after death you will still be alive and looking back with joy or sorrow upon the chances you have taken or have missed? That is the question. But I think it is natural for people to ask, since it is the question, and since the issue is so important, why on earth we do not find more definite and detailed information about that other world within the pages of Holy Writ. Christ must have known, but why did He not tell us? It would have made us so much more certain, so much more sure of our ground, it would have been such an enormous comfort to people in sorrow, to know not merely that in His Father's House there were many mansions, but what the mansions were like, what people did there, and what they wore, and the kind of life they lived. He might have told us, but He passed on, only uttering the words of hope and warning, 'More life with Me or without.' It is this natural longing that in these last days since the war, when the many mansions of that other world have suddenly become filled with a multitude of young and ardent spirits who leapt into it from the battle-field, has given rise to a revival of curiosity and longing to know more, and hence a great revival of interest in the possibility and means of communication between this world and the next.

All down history, from the very earliest times, there has been found among men, sometimes waxing and sometimes waning, the belief that communication with the departed was possible and actually took place. There is no older belief in the world than belief in ghosts. The literature and folklore of every people are full of ghost stories, but in modern days it has become for the first time possible, owing to the increased rapidity of communication, the invention of printing, and mutual understanding of different tongues, to gather all this evidence together; hitherto it has been scattered and impossible to collect. Now an enormous volume of such evidence has been gathered, and for years men have been at work upon it, endeavouring to estimate its value on scientific lines, and come to some definite conclusion as to what it all means. Are all these stories the results of disordered imagination and of queer tricks that our sub-conscious selves can play? Are they all due to fraud and deception, or is it true that off and on we do hear a knocking at the door? I cannot claim to be an expert, and perhaps it is only the opinion of experts in this matter which is worth anything, but for my part I rise from my studies with the feeling that it is impossible to dismiss all the evidence as either imaginary or fraudulent, and very difficult to believe it to be all due to the queer tricks of the sub-conscious mind. All those factors enter in and make the judgment more difficult. There is madness, there is fraud and deception, and there are queer tricks of the sub-conscious self; but when we have allowed for all that, it seems to me as if there was something more. But the whole body of evidence with regard to the nature of the other world contains almost nothing satisfying or satisfactory that one can rely upon. Every supposed communication has to be examined and tested, and probably a great part of it has to be rejected for one cause or another, and it seems to be practically impossible for an ordinary person to arrive at any certain element of truth, although he may have a very strong impression that there is an element of truth there. All our research does not seem to have lifted the veil that Christ let down between that world and this.

The best summary of the conclusions at which one arrives is that given to me by a friend who has been investigating psychic phenomena for many years. 'I believe that the evidence for survival and the possibility of communication as against the negative evidence just balances over on the positive side, and I believe in both. But as to the worth of the communications with regard to the nature of the other world, they are about equal to the following: They are as if an Eskimo who had just landed in India were endeavouring to tell an Eskimo who had never been to India over a telephone service forty times as bad as the National Telephone Service is, what India was like, provided the one in India had delirium tremens.'

The veil is not lifted, and we do not know. If a person really understands the tremendous difficulties that lie in the way of proving any given message valid, I think the knowledge ought to be sufficient to convince him that this is a matter for trained people to investigate in a highly sceptical and scientific spirit, and not a point at which ordinary fools can break in where angels fear to tread. This is an unsatisfying and non-committal sort of conclusion, but I believe it is the truth. I do not believe that there is any solid or real gain to be gotten out of amateur experiments in Spiritualism. I do not believe that Christ's silence has been really broken yet, nor do I believe that any good can come to the ordinary run of His children by their trying to break it. It may be that more light will come, it may be that Christ intends to break the silence, but it is quite clear that the dangers which attend any but trained and careful people in trying to pass beyond the veil are tremendous, and that for the ordinary man or woman it is far better to rest back upon the fundamental fact which Christ taught (and which is strengthened and confirmed by the truth that there is in this conflicting mass of evidence), that there is the other world, and that our fate there depends upon our life here.

The result of the ordinary person taking up with enthusiasm the investigation of this evidence and the practice of communication through automatic writing, séances, etc., is either that they simply disregard all the intense and complicated difficulties that beset the communication and lay themselves open to wholesale deception, and live in a fool's paradise. which real knowledge might at any moment cause to come tumbling about their ears, or else that they produce in their minds, *not a tremendous certainty, but a maddening doubt.*

There are, of course, exceptions. There is a tremendous certainty in Sir Arthur Conan Doyle's words: -

'It was granted me to stand
By my dead,
I have felt the vanished hand
On my head,
On my brow the vanished lips,
And I know that death's eclipse
Is a floating veil that slips
Or is shed.

G A Studdert Kennedy

'When I heard thy well-known voice,
Son of mine,
Should I silently rejoice
Or incline
To strike harder as a fighter
That the heavy might be lighter,
That the gloomy might be brighter
At the sign?'

But in thousands of cases the result is not that, but rather a dreadful doubt.

'Is this so well-known voice
That speaks
Just as he used to do of yore,
With just that turning of the words,
Is it some trick of my sub-conscious self
And nothing more,
Or is it truth,
That from some other world
My love is knocking at the door?

'I could have sworn it was his voice
That spoke, it woke
So many sweet responsive echoes
In my soul
And stole across my senses
As his voice was wont to do
In thrills of golden joy.

'And yet, and yet
It may be that I can't forget
Because he lives in me,
And through and through
My soul is drenched with his,
And memory
Plays some wild jest.

'Dear God, wouldst Thou permit
So vile a lie
To trick a poor forsaken heart,
And break the rest,
The troubled rest,
That time allows me from my grief?
But why should this be viler
Than the million lies

> That lure men to destruction every day?
> So many stars are lit
> Up in the sky
> That lead men nowhere
> But to some grey
> Dawn of sorrow and a barren shore,
> Where nought remains of their dead dream
> But an exceeding bitter cry,
> And that cry's echo "Nevermore."'

That is often and often the result, and that way madness lies. It does seem to be perfectly certain that it is at their peril that ordinary men and women substitute this everlasting probing into the future for a brave, unswerving faith that neither in life nor death can ought of real evil happen to those who put their trust in God, and seek for love as it is in Jesus.

But there is more still behind this clause, there surrounds it a Christian tradition that the Spirit of Jesus, when it passed on to Paradise, was not idle there and did not sleep, but spread abroad in Paradise, as He spread abroad on earth, the great good news of God's Eternal Love and of Salvation yet to come. Whether it was that our Lord told St. Peter this after He was risen from the Tomb, or whether it was just that the Christians who knew Christ felt that this was a necessity that followed from the Love of God as they had found it revealed in Him, because otherwise all the countless millions of men and women who had lived and died before He walked upon the earth, and lived His Life, and died His Death to bring new Life into the world, would have been ignorant and in the dark, and would have remained without hope of salvation, eternally lost - whether, I say, the tradition sprang from Christ Himself or sprang from the meditations of Christians upon the Love of God revealed in Christ, it stands there as part of the great Gospel, and it does seem to be legitimate for us to draw conclusions from it. I conclude that Christ passed into Paradise to meet not only the repentant thief, but the unrepentant thief as well. He went to preach to those that were sometime disobedient because, for reasons beyond their power to control, they had never seen Christ. The reason in their case was that they were not born in time, but there are a million other reasons that operate in the world to prevent men ever seeing Christ, reasons which are beyond their power to control. Thousands of men and women have lived since Jesus died, and never known His Name. The line sweeps out to the ends of the world, East and West, and North and South, and gathers the staggering multitude in, black and white, red and yellow, old and young, and the message of the Cross comes for them; neither length nor breadth, nor depth nor height, nor death itself, can separate them from the love of Christ which passes knowledge. Even beyond the grave there is hope. The God of Life goes on striving in the after world; death is a crisis, but not an ending. In our own towns and cities and villages are there not thousands born in rotten slums, their bodies tainted with disease, their minds debauched by the corruption of great cities, feeble-minded, vicious, half-insane? What is to become of them? It is no good trying to believe that they can grasp the Gospel, or that they have eyes to see. It is comfortable to believe it, but it does not tally with facts. If any slum worker tries to work, believing that death ends the opportunity of life, and that either a man must be brought now or never to the knowledge of God, it will break his heart.

There are those who simply cannot respond, and for them the message comes that He passed into Paradise, and that just as the Crucifixion is an act in time, revealing a process in Eternity, so is the descent into Hell. Just as it is true not merely that He suffered once, but that He suffers still to save mankind. Just as it is true that

'Red with His Blood, the better day is dawning
Pierced by His pain, the storm-clouds roll apart;
Rings o'er the earth the message of the morning,
Still on the Cross the Saviour bears His Heart.

'Passionate and low, the voice of God is pleading,
Pleading with men to arm them for the fight,
See how those Hands, majestically bleeding,
Call us to rout the armies of the night.'

So it is true not merely that He descended once into Hell, but that He for ever descends to the depths to seek and to save that which is lost, and that

'His Love is an unchanging Love,
Higher than the heights above,
Deeper than the depths beneath,
Free and faithful, strong as death,'

and stronger.

Once more this clause rings out the challenge to the belief in the everlasting Love, and calls us out upon the journey, upwards and onwards through life and through death, to the Jesus order of goodness, following the Star of Bethlehem that set on Calvary's hill only to rise and shine again more brightly as the lodestar of the human race.

There is no positive proof, there is nothing that *can compel certainty,* about the existence of that other world. There are a multitude of arguments from the nature of consciousness itself, and from the relation of the mind to the body, which tend to make its existence *probable,* and which tend to make it reasonable for us to bet upon it as a truth, but it remains a venture of faith. And so once more the gallant Creed calls us to stake our lives upon the great chance, and to live on the assumption that God will not leave us in the grave, nor suffer His children to see corruption, but that we shall pass on to Paradise.

XI. *The Third Day He rose again from the dead*

TO the convinced Christian - the man who has really burned his boats behind him and set out to seek for Life as it is in Jesus - the most thrilling day in the whole year is Easter Day. It brings to him a joy that is like no other joy that life affords, all other experiences fade before it. If the chorus of earth's billion voices, with the roll of ten thousand drums, could crash out together in a song of praise, it would not be worthy unless it were joined with the voices of angels and archangels and the whole company of Heaven.

Of course, that is not an argument, not a formal or logical argument, but I doubt if it is not *the* argument - the argument of vivid experience against which oceans of logic and seas of pure cold reason might break and break in vain. Fresh like the Spring it comes again each year with its abounding gladness.

I have not had a sad life; the world has been good to me, most of the joys of the common day I have tasted and found good. I have loved the sunshine, felt the call of Mother Earth, thrilled to the beauty of sunset skies, and known the quiet peace of home. I have been young, and known the joys of youth, and have answered with all my heart to the poet's call -

'How good is man's life, the mere living, how fit to employ
All the heart and the soul and the senses for ever enjoy,'

and yet I am prepared honestly and soberly to state that I know no joy like that of Easter Day.

'Have I not lived and known the joys of living,
Bathed in its sunshine, wandered in its rain,
Have I not known the glories of self-giving,
The pleasures that plead and pierce the soul like pain?

Have I not loved and drunk the wine of passion,
Thrilled to a smile and swooned beneath a kiss?
Yet were they feeble and powerless to fashion
Splendours that burn, realities like this.'

Here, in this year of grace 1920, I still find in the Resurrection of my Lord the quintessence of all that makes life supremely well worth living. It is very difficult to probe and analyse this experience either in oneself or as it appears in the Christians of all time, but it certainly means more than just the conviction that the soul survives death could possibly bring. Easter Day means more to me, and always has meant to Christians more, than just the certainty that death is not the end of life. It does not merely bring to me the message of a longer life, it brings the message of a new kind of life altogether; it is not merely that it opens the gates of death and lets me into a new world after this; it is that it abolishes death altogether and opens out a new world which includes this - a world in which the sunshine is more golden and the fields more vivid green, and in which the flowers of God's beauty never really fade away. That is how it is with me, and in that I seem to stand in with all other Christians. The Risen Christ has always brought to us not merely release from the death of the body as a thing to fear and dread, but release from the death of the soul, a conviction of at any rate potential freedom from slavery to sin.

It is very difficult, if you sit down to study St. Paul's letters, to make out, when he is talking about death, whether he means the death of the body or the death of the soul. This was perhaps because in his case the two things were one, and he may have believed that for every one who did not find Christ death was the end of all things; but it was certainly also because he always thought about death, not as anything which happened to the body, but as the climax of sin and separation from God, and so the Resurrection to him meant not merely that he would be conscious after death, and that his personality would survive, but that he was set free from slavery to sin here and now. If Christ be not risen, the dreadful consequence is not that death ends life, but that we are still in our sins, still the slaves of lust and hatred and envy, jealousy, and greed. To the first Christians the great meaning of the Resurrection was that in the Risen Christ they found not merely an assurance of survival in another world, but a Saviour Who set them free from the slavery in this, and that is what the Resurrection still means to Christian men and women. It is the same joy that links us down the ages, and yet perhaps not quite the same. You see, to these first Christians it was a perfect and completed thing. In the first flush of their enthusiasm, while they still believed that in a very short time the Lord would come again and gather up His own, they were convinced that this new freedom from the power of evil was meant to be a constant and lasting experience. They found it difficult to believe that sin committed after entry on the new life could be forgiven; they were convinced that they had passed from death unto life because they loved the brethren, and that in this perfect, sinless Fellowship of His Church they would be able to live until He came in clouds and glory, and took His power to reign.

We cannot understand the Resurrection Gospel of the first Christians unless we remember constantly that it was largely based upon and linked up with a firm conviction that within a very few years the trumpets of the angels would announce the Second Coming. To them the Cross was finished, final, and complete. It was as empty as the Empty Tomb. Redemption was an accomplished fact, they were dead unto sin, freed altogether from its power, transformed and made al: over again, new creatures. The winter of sin and sorrow was past, the rain of tears had become the sunshine of perpetual joy, and flowers of perfect goodness appeared at last upon the earth; the time of the singing-birds was come, and the voice of the turtle-dove of perfect peace was heard iii the land.

It was that experience of completed redemption and release which sent the first preachers of the Christ to tell the great good news to the peoples of the world, with hearts of love and tongues of flame. But since those days floods and floods of water have flowed beneath the bridges of the world - floods of evil-smelling, dirty water, foul with corruption and sin. Christ still delays His coming, and His children have not been faithful to their trust. The powers of evil have not been vanquished, and the worm of sin has eaten its way into the heart of the Brotherhood itself.

The history of the two thousand years that have passed since Jesus rose again is a dark and terrible business. There are no words that could do justice to that awful picture, to the horrors of its everlasting wars, its oppressions, persecutions, cruelties, lies; down the pathway of the years man comes fighting fierce with bloody hands, and stands at last in these last days, looking out through blinding tears across the barren desert that was once the smiling valley of the Somme.

The history of the Brotherhood itself is full of sin and shame. Christ's Name has been made a war-cry, and under the banner of His Cross men have marched to pillage and to burn, to murder women and torture children, and to trample tenderness and beauty underfoot. It is impossible that, looking back at the Cross and the Empty Tomb through the darkness of these hideous years, we should see them as the first Christians saw them. It is not any use to tell us that one thousand years in God's sight are but as yesterday when it has passed, and as a watch in the night. Time may be nothing to God, but surely sin and sorrow are much. It is not the time, but the sin of the years that makes us see the truth in a different light. To us the Cross cannot be empty, we dare not think of it thus, it has been too often repeated, and it is repeated still; its shadow still falls darkly across the fairest scenes in all the world. To us redemption cannot be a completed and a finished thing. We cannot blind our eyes to the fact that every day and every hour of every day Christ is crucified afresh. But if the Cross is still there, and if its shadow does fall across the world, what we can and do assert is that the sunshine of the Resurrection is there too, and it is that which makes the shadow so black and so distinct. The first fine flush of Christian enthusiasm may fade, but it has not faded away, and it has not left darkness behind; there is still the Light of the world. We cannot see the Cross and the Resurrection as two distinct and finished acts; we see them as one - one great act in time revealing a process of Eternity, revealing the Love of the suffering but triumphant God. We see redemption, not as a finished and completed thing, but as a purpose that is being worked out, and is to be completed in the fullness of God's time. So we see it in ourselves, and so we see it in the world. We cannot say of ourselves that we are dead to sin and alive only to goodness; we cannot say that it is no longer we that live, but Christ that liveth in us, that we are new creatures; we cannot say that the Cross in our own hearts is empty, that we are risen with Him; but what we can and do say is that we are dying to sin, that Christ is crucified every day, but that He rises again, that in our lives He is suffering, but we are filled with the conviction that He is to be triumphant, that He has gotten a hold on us, and will not let us go, that although He is but feeble, is as it were just a baby in a manger, hidden away in the poorest room in the crowded inn of our lives, He makes us feel that He is to be one day the Lord of Glory, the King of Kings. That is how we see Christ crucified and risen again in ourselves, and that is how we see Him in the world and in the Church - crucified - crucified in every street of our great cities, crucified in every hovel of our slums, crucified on our markets, crucified on our battle-fields, but for ever rising again. Again and again men cry that He is dead and buried, antiquated, impossible, mythical; again and again He comes back, takes hold on human hearts, and sends them out to preach His truth, aflame with the old new Love. Once more we see how the great idea of the moving universe - the idea of progress and development - comes in to throw new light and make a wonderful harmony of the apparent contradictions of Christian experience. Looked at in the light of that idea, the old old story takes once more the powers of youth and goes out to win the young. If our Gospel were only a Gospel of the Crucified, it would be untrue to facts and a Gospel of despair. But the Gospel of the Cross and the Empty Tomb, of the Crucified Risen Christ, always crucified and always rising again, is the Gospel that faces all facts and gives to life a meaning.

There is in the heart of God, and always has been, a Cross and an Empty Tomb.

It is to the search for this experience that the great clause, 'And on the third day He rose again from the dead,' challenges mankind. But there is a question which will be in the hearts of all of us men to ask, 'How far was this experience bound up, and how far must it always be bound up, with belief in the miracle - the stark-naked miracle - of the Empty Tomb?' And when we come to this it is as though we stood once more before the Manger in Bethlehem and asked, 'Is it true that He was born of the Virgin Mary?' These are the two great miracles.

Standing before the Empty Tomb is like standing before the Manger of Bethlehem. Just the same doubts and just the same difficulties beset us in these modern days as we contemplate these two bewildering mysteries of Christ's Birth and Resurrection. There is just the same conflict of duties - the duty of faith strives in the honest man's mind with the duty of doubt. There is much that bids him believe, and much that bids him hesitate before he permits himself to believe. It is not, and it ought not to be, easy for us to accept a miracle. We have learnt to our great gain to seek for God in the ordinary rather than in the extraordinary, in the common rather than in the rare things of life. We have passed from the stage when men declared that miracles were impossible. We would not say anything was impossible, because we know that our knowledge of the resources of the universe is infinitely small; we do not feel inclined to go blundering, like fools, with dogmatic assertions into places where men of decent intelligence - never mind the angels - are afraid to tread. We cannot reject all miracles, but neither can we accept all. We cannot see any virtue in a faith which defies and sets at nought the claims of truth. The first question that any honest man must ask about a doctrine is whether it is true or not, and as to the actual occurrence of this miracle - for miracle it is - we have to go upon evidence. But the evidence for the Resurrection is very much stronger than the evidence for the Virgin Birth. There is absolutely no doubt whatever that it was accepted and believed by every Christian from the very beginning, and was the foundation of their whole faith; it is otherwise with the Virgin Birth. It is not certain whether St. Paul or St. John believed in the Virgin Birth, it is plumb certain that they believed in the Resurrection, practically certain that they believed in the Empty Tomb and the disappearance of the Body.

It is difficult indeed to make a consistent whole of the Gospel story of the Resurrection, and there seems to be little doubt that legends grew up around it - earthquakes and glistening angels; but, allowing for that element, there is very strong evidence that the earliest Christians firmly believed on the testimony of eye-witnesses that the Tomb was empty and the Body not to be seen, and there is no doubt that the full Resurrection experience of the early Christians was bound up with that belief. It is not certain that their experience was equally bound up with belief in the Virgin Birth.

It seems to follow, then, that the Resurrection experience, the enthusiasm and the fire that burned in the early Church, the sudden transformation of the scattered and bewildered little band whose hopes had been blasted by the Cross into a united and serenely confident company of missionaries, prepared to face death for their living Lord, can be taken as some evidence for the truth of what they believed. It seems to me to be conclusive evidence that something astounding happened, and that they did see Christ, and did actually talk with Him, and did actually touch Him, and never forgot it. Unless I believe that, the story of the early Church, and indeed the whole subsequent history of Europe, seems intolerably difficult to explain. Something astounding happened. Men talked with Jesus, touched Him, after death, and that experience changed their whole lives. Was it really a miracle - a unique and solitary intervention of God - or was it something which, in the fullness of the years, we shall learn to understand? Is it in any way parallel with other appearances and other communications with the departed which are recorded in history and vouched for by eye-witnesses? That I simply do not know. But I do say this, that if it was proved to be so, it would not make a whit of difference to my faith. The Resurrection experience is not bound up for me with the technically miraculous nature of the

Resurrection itself. The Christian Faith for me is all bound up in the fact that the Cross was not the end, that Christ appeared upon the earth again, that He was seen and spoken to by men, but it is not bound up with the belief that in the fullness of time no man would ever do that again. Resurrections might become commonplace, and Christ's Resurrection still remain unique.

I cannot say as yet, nor does it seem to me that any one can say with certainty, how far the Resurrection of our Lord was a real stark-naked miracle, and how far it runs actually parallel to other recorded experiences of communications with the dead. It is quite clear that there was something odd about the Resurrection Body of our Lord, about its appearances and disappearances. It is quite clear that His Life with His disciples after the Resurrection was not the same completely normal and natural communion as was His Life before His Death, and when He appeared to the five hundred brethren at once, there were some that doubted it. But whatever it was that actually occurred, it seems to me sufficiently certain that a real objective Christ came back and talked with men, and on that fact the Resurrection experience of the first Christians was based. The evidence for that fact seems to me to grow stronger every day as the effects of that conviction grow greater, as the Carpenter of Nazareth strengthens His hold on the hearts of men, and the Gospel of His Life and Death and Resurrection seems to light up with a clearer and clearer meaning the history of the world. The fact of the Living Christ grows larger and larger, and demands more insistently that it should have a sufficient cause. Each Easter Day adds to the wonder of the first, and makes it seem less and less probable that this tremendous human experience can be based upon pure delusion.

The Christian Faith is, as it were, the monument of the Resurrection; it stands as a deathless witness to the Deathlessness of Christ. The world abounds with stories of risen saviours and conquerors of death, and in every people of the world almost there is a story of one who went through the Valley of the Shadow and came back with news that all was well; and to me that points to the fact that, unless the world was made by a mocking devil, there was One who really did fulfil the prophecy that arose spontaneously in the hearts of men wherever the sun made night and day. And so it comes to this. I believe that it happened, I believe that 'on the third day He rose again from the dead.' As to how it happened, as to whether it was an absolute miracle or something that in the days to come, as we know more of Him, we shall grow to understand, I do not know. I wish I did, perhaps some day I shall - who knows? Life is long, very long, there is no death - it is Eternal - I shall know Him as He is.

Meanwhile, I find in the Risen Christ the assurance of Eternal Life, the knowledge that I am now the son of God, and have in Him the present power of Salvation from my sin.

XII.   *He ascended into Heaven*

DID He? Where is Heaven? What is it? Is it a place? Is it a spiritual condition? Can we know what it is, or where it is? God is Spirit, without body, parts, or passions. What do you mean by 'Sitteth at the right hand of God the Father'? You cannot mean it literally because He has not got a hand. You cannot mean that He literally sat down. Do you mean that He literally went up? Is this history or allegory? Did He really ascend? Was there ever a day or night when that small band stood with upturned faces gazing into the clouds and straining their eyes to catch a glimpse of the slowly disappearing Figure with hands outstretched to bless them in His last farewell? And suppose He did go up into the Heavens, suppose it was an actual case of self-levitation, what difference does it make to you or me? It is an extraordinary story, and if it is a fact it is a very interesting fact, and calls for careful scientific investigation and a search to see if any similar cases are recorded in history, and if there are, to study their common features with a view to finding out what general law governs such occurrences. There is, of course, Elijah going up in a whirlwind into Heaven, but that is not very certain history, is it? It does not really help us very much. And, altogether apart from the question of fact, why should it be considered necessary for my soul's health in this year 1920, to believe that Jesus Christ disappeared from this earth almost two thousand years ago by an act of self-levitation, and went upwards into space until He was out of sight? Granted for the moment that He did do it, what odds does it make to me now, or to anybody else? Does it matter whether I believe it as a fact or treat it as a beautiful legend? Of course, I don't deny its beauty; I think the pictures of the Ascension are amongst the most inspiring and exalting that great art has ever given us - but does it matter to me and to the world whether this actually happened or not?

Here are two distinct questions. Did it happen? and what difference does it make if it did?

Let us get down to the first. Did it happen? did He ascend? The only evidence that we have for the picture which is so familiar and so gloriously beautiful - the picture of that dear and well-beloved Figure rising slowly from the earth, with pierced hands held out in everlasting benediction - the only evidence we have for it is the testimony of St. Luke. St. John does not give it, nor does St. Matthew; the end of St. Mark was not written by St. Mark, and it does not give the picture, only just the fact, 'He was taken up into Heaven and sat down at the right hand of God,' the second part of which is evidently symbolic, so why not the first? It is St. Luke in the Acts of the Apostles who has given us the picture. Is it true?

How can I tell for certain? How can any one tell? If one is to approach the question coldly, and in a sceptical spirit, remembering the honest man's duty of doubt, it seems to me that the only conclusion we can come to upon the evidence is that it cannot be proved. The evidence is not sufficiently strong to convince a reasonable and impartial person approaching the matter in a purely scientific spirit.

Well, does not that give the whole show away? That is what I have always felt, you say, ever since I was a child. The Christian Creed won't wash or wear. When you plunge it into the cold water of reason it shrinks until there is nothing left of it, nothing save this splendid but shadowy Figure Who fades away into the mists of time, and leaves us alone with wars and workhouses, factory chimneys and squalid streets - alone in a modern mechanical, vulgar world of sordid realities. O my God, these tales of unbearable beauty that break the hearts of men because they are not true! I came out of Birmingham Cathedral, from the Burne-Jones window of the Ascension, into the twilight streets, and an amateur prostitute giggled. The oldest profession in the world - dreams and reality. Bother your beastly questions. If it is a dream, why need you come in with your vulgarity and spit on your fingers to turn it over and examine it? I am sick of your book and your honesty. Do we not need our dreams? I have never asked myself these questions before, and why need I ask them at all? Better men than you have believed it without question, and who are you to doubt them? Go and say your prayers, and ask God to strengthen your faith.

That's one me. But there is another that answers, 'Please, I don't want to be vulgar, and I don't want to be blatant. I don't want to ask questions, but the beastly things ask themselves. They kept on asking themselves while I was saying my prayers. Is it true? How do you know it is? Isn't it only a fool's paradise this faith of yours? You have only St. Luke for it, and it is a strange and unique occurrence. You must be honest first and religious afterwards - you know you must. You know the horrors that come if you twist those things the wrong way round - orthodox lies for the glory of God. It's no use, you must be honest first.' Of course, there are more things in Heaven or earth than are dreamed of in your philosophy or any one else's, if it comes to that, but then the fact that anything may be true is no proof that any one thing is. The fact that Christ may have ascended does not prove that He did; you have no evidence that will convince an impartial intellect, and that ends it.

But does it? I doubt if intellect ever ends it. It is not big enough. You cannot take this story and cut it off from all the rest, isolate it and put it under the microscope of historical criticism, and then decide that there is nothing in it. You cannot get at the real truth of it that way, you would only get the same result as a chemist would who analysed the Sistine Madonna and expressed it in chemical formula; it would be truth of a sort, but not the truth; it would be an abstract truth, which, like lawyers' truth, is often another name for lies. You see, it is palpable, blunder-headed nonsense to say that a picture is only canvas and paint; it is plainly and obviously a great deal more than that. The reality in a picture is the power that draws and moulds men's minds, that haunts and grips their thoughts; the reality of the picture is the personality of the painter. That is what it really is. A great song is not a series of atmospheric vibrations causing molecular changes in the matter of the brain, it is laughter and tears, it is joy and sorrow, it is life itself, it is a person calling to a person, a heart that seeks a heart. It is hard to put these things into words, but you understand what I mean, don't you? This Ascension picture is not merely itself - bald, isolated, historical fact; the reality of the Ascension picture is the Personality of the Ascending Christ. Before we can properly weigh and estimate the value of the evidence for its reality we must have some understanding of that Personality.

You must take up the Christian challenge in its due order, you cannot swallow it whole, it will give you indigestion, mental, moral, and spiritual stomach-ache; before you decide about the Ascension of Christ you must decide about Christ Himself. Who and what was He - a myth? a magician? a man? the Perfect Man? a God? You must start where those who lived and died for their Ascended Lord started, face to face with Jesus. You must have seen Jesus before you can see the Ascending and Ascended Christ. You must have set out to follow Him, and you must have found Him at once inevitable, impossible, and infectious - in a word, Divine. You must have found Him in your own soul, crucified, continually crucified, and yet rising again, before you can grasp the meaning of His Ascension. You can only pass through Good Friday and Easter Day to your Ascension-tide. It is no mere put-off that. You must know what a man was, what his power and his character was, before you can rightly judge about the truth or falsehood of an event recorded in his life. What might quite well happen to one person might be utterly impossible for another.

There is always the factor of personality to be reckoned with in estimating historical reality. If I did not believe that Jesus Christ was like no other person that ever lived, if I did not believe that He was unique, the one and only, this story would have no reality for me; it would be as the fairy tales, shadow without substance, which is a sickening diet for working men. But if you have entered into the challenge thus far, if you have taken up the life and the struggle it demands, if you have set out on the great adventure, it makes a whole lot of difference. The reality of the story will then become more and more an absolute necessity for you. I know that that is an argument with a double edge. That is just it, you say, that is how it all came about. These early Christians had taken up the life, they had fallen under the spell of the great illusion, 'The King had bound them by such vows as were a shame a man should not be bound by, yet the which no man can keep,' and being under that illusion, and bound by such vows, the story became a necessity to them, and they invented it. That is a 'natural reply, and if you can still believe that the Christian life is a great illusion, and that there is no reality behind it, if you can still believe that Christianity is one of the great world lies, and that Christian hopes and longings are all destined to end in disappointment, then I do not think there is any chance that you will be able to find any reality in this story. In that case we must go back before we can go on. We must go back and stand before the Character and ask ourselves again, What about it? What about Him? I believe in the Ascension because of Christ. I do not believe in Christ because of the Ascension.

The thing is this. Across the ages, when I take up the New Testament, I find myself talking with men who knew Some One that I know, who loved Some One that I love, and who worshipped Some One that I worship. This Person, as far as this world was concerned, was a dead failure. His earthly career fizzled out upon the Cross. He was like a Very light shot up into the sky, dazzling the eye with its brilliance, and then dying away to leave a deeper darkness behind. They all knew that, these men. They all knew that from a worldly point of view His Life was one succession of failures, that His career was as unlike that of the Messiah the people expected as it well could be - He could not even get twelve entirely faithful followers. Yet I find these men calmly confident that He was and is the One Supreme success, that in Him, and in Him alone, there is no failure but complete and perfect triumph. How did He succeed in producing this impression upon them? St. Luke may be the only one who records the picture, but he is not by any means the only one who records the impression. That is universal among Christians. How did it become so? He went away and left them - left them to fight it out apparently by themselves, and they did not have such a blazing good time either. The whole world did not fall upon their necks and embrace them as saviours, they had a job to get on at all. The Church they built was not such a howling success, it was a poor struggling thing. Yet these men and women remained unshaken in their confidence that it had the root of the matter in it, because He was in it and with it always until the end of the world.

How did they come by this conviction? Why were they not cast down and brokenhearted when He left them? Why were they not plunged into the depths of despair as they were after the Crucifixion? The answer that they gave was that although He went away, the manner of His going was such that it convinced them that all was well, that He would come again, and that meanwhile they would not be left alone and leaderless, but that in some new way He would be with them still. The manner of His going was not like a retreat., but like an advance; it spoke of victory, and not defeat. It was not a departure, it was an ascension, it was the revelation of what He was - equal with God. They were not down-hearted, because Jesus was with God, and God was with them, and could never leave them.

That is their account of how it was they were not down-hearted, but bubbling over with excitement and expectation. Christ had fought, and

Christ had won; in Him was victory. That was the universal Christian impression. Whether St. Luke gives an exact and accurate account of the way in which that impression was produced, or whether he gives the traditional picture in which Christ's followers were wont to express the impression made upon them by His departure, cannot, I believe, be decided with certainty on the evidence we have. I think it is the simplest and easiest supposition to go upon, that the picture is substantially accurate, but whether it is or not, it is certain that it describes in the most vivid and compelling fashion the convictions that His departure created in the minds of those who witnessed it. He went away triumphant and to come again. It was an ascension, not a failure and farewell. That is certain, and that is the main thing. The manner in which the conviction was created is not so important, the conviction that this is the victory that overcometh the world, even our faith, that is all-important, and it is, and always has been, the essence of Christianity. But you may say, Yes, I know the impression of victory is the main thing, but was it not a false impression, were not these early Christians confident that He would come again quite soon, were they not expecting that the Second Coming was only a matter of months, or at most of a few years? You mention that in your chapter on the Resurrection - the expectation of a Second Coming quite soon; and has not that expectation proved to be a fizzle too? You see He has not come, and there are no real signs of His Coming. They thought He would come again within a year or two, come in clouds of glory, and take His power to reign, and we look around the world and see only this after the Passion of two thousand years. The promise of His Second Coming has not been fulfilled. They were mistaken, those early Christians, they were mistaken about this. How can we be sure that they were not mistaken about His Ascension too? How can we be sure that it was not just a legend which grew up to express their early enthusiasm and buoy them up in their false hopes? To them the Ascension evidently meant the completed, final triumph of Christ. His work was done, His sorrow ended, His redemption of the world an accomplished fact. Can it mean that to us? To them His return to Heaven was like the return of an Eastern conqueror, with sin and death as captives in His train.

'To meet Him all His saints, who silent stood
Eye-witnesses of His Almighty acts,
With jubilee advanced, and as they went,
Shaded with branching palm, each order bright
Sung triumph and Him, sung Victorious King,
Son, heir, and Lord, to Him dominion give,
Worthiest to reign. He celebrated rode
Triumphant through mid-heaven into the courts
And temple of His Mighty Father, throned
On high, Who unto glory Him received,
Where now He sits at the right hand of Bliss.'

That is what it meant to them. Can it mean that to us? Can we regard His task as accomplished and His triumph as complete when

> 'Here on the earth as years pass by,
> Centuries piled upon Calvary,
> The story of man is but one long line
> Of insults heaped on the plan Divine.
> Murder and misery, rape and war,
> Sin like an open, festering sore,
> Oozing its filth through the souls of men,
> Dragging them down to the dust again,
> Worming its way through their noblest deeds,
> Burying God in their Godless creeds.
> Priests that spit in the face of Christ,
> Cardinals decked for the traitorous tryst
> They keep with a God their souls despise,
> For the policy's sake of the worldly wise.
> Children conceived and born in sin,
> Rotten with syphilis, soaked in gin,
> Housed like pigs in their filthy stys,
> Cursed from the day they opened their eyes.'

Is not this triumph of Christ a mockery? Is not this victory which was assured to the first Christians by the manner of His departure a lie? Does it not look as if the whole conception was an illusion and the New Testament merely the story of a great human hope that history has killed as it has killed a million other splendid hopes, and will probably kill a million more?

> 'How can it be that Christ can reign in glory,
> Calmly content with what His love has done,
> Reading unmoved the piteous, shameful story
> Of the vile deeds men do beneath the sun?'

If Christ is the same yesterday, to-day, and for ever, then His soul must be wrung now as it was wrung in the days of His flesh, as He looks down upon the world as it is to-day. Once more these two thousand years must make a difference. We cannot disregard them. Once more, I say, time may be nothing to God, but if He is a reality at all, sin must be much, and these two thousand years have been two thousand years of sin - of sin and suffering beyond the power of any words to compass or express. If they change for us the Resurrection experience, they must change for us the Ascension experience too. It cannot be for us a perfect and completed thing; we are bound to see it against a different background - against the background of the two thousand years. History has done its worst, done its very damnedest, to kill the hope, to destroy the faith, and rob us of our certainty, but once again the gallant Creed rings out its note of defiance. It has not killed the hope, it cries; the hope, nay, more, the calm and confident certainty, still burns and blazes in the hearts of those who have found God in Christ. To them the final reality of life is perfectly expressed in Christ Crucified, Risen, and Ascending, with hands outstretched to bless them. That is what they see everywhere. They do not see Him regnant on a great white throne, with all His work behind Him, and all His sorrow done - they know He sorrows now, as He did then - but they do see Him as the equal of the Highest, the expression, the very image, of what the Power behind life is. If they look into their own souls they find Him there - crucified, but deathless and ascending - Christ in them the Hope of Glory, bound to triumph in the end. If they look at the history of the world with its struggle and its strife and its sin, they find Him, once more crucified, but deathless and ascending, slowly but surely coming to His own, irresistibly moving to the accomplishment of His purpose. We do not presume to pierce beyond the veil to regions that we do not know, to truths beyond those which the Incarnation has revealed. We do not any longer draw imaginary pictures of splendid courts and glistening thrones, of perfect songs of triumph unbroken by a discord or a flaw. We do not venture to give Christ in Heaven what He never would have on earth, the symbols of material power. We are content with the picture that has been given us, the picture of the dear and well-beloved Figure with the pierced hands, slowly rising upwards into regions out of sight, and that picture makes all history luminous. History is not the story of the descent of man from the apes, but the ascent of God in Man to the Angels. We believe in the Risen and Ascending Christ, and we find evidence of it everywhere.

Had we clung fast to the Truth revealed in the Ascension, the Revelation of the meaning of Life and History that it contains, the new knowledge of God's method of creation by evolution might have been for us a pure and unmixed blessing. We would never have allowed ourselves to look down to the beasts for the meaning of life as we did, we would have remained steadfastly gazing up into Heaven. We would never have been deceived into thinking that because we were descended from the jungle, therefore the laws of the jungle must govern our lives for ever. We would never have allowed the blasphemy to be spread abroad that strife, struggle, war, and remorseless competition were the laws of God. The blight of pseudo-scientific cant would never have ruined our social lives. We would have known that evolution was not a descent but an ascension, not a mechanical and determined ascension, but a moral and spiritual progress which can only take place as men are in Christ, living their life in His Spirit, and basing their thought on His law - the law of Love. Had we clung fast to the Ascending Christ, and refused to surrender His truth to Godless economists, there might have been no Manchester school, and no slums, no Treitschke, no Nietzsche, and no battle of the Somme. We might before now have succeeded in building the New Jerusalem in this island home of ours.

We have forsaken the Truth and paid the inevitable penalty, but let us return to it now.

There is in it power to heal the gaping wounds of war.

We can turn away from that picture, and with its truth as our great treasure firm and fast we can honestly face the facts of life, and stare them in the face, and defy their power to hurt or harm, in the power of the Ascending Christ.

XIII. And shall come again at the end of the world to judge the quick and the dead

WHEN will He come? Will He ever come? Isn't it all moonshine? Will there ever be a Day of Judgment - a day when all the nations of the world shall stand in their teeming millions before the Great White Throne, and hear their final sentence read, and know their fate is fixed for all eternity?

There is no doubt that the early Christians based their lives upon the certainty of that Second Coming and of the great judgment, and believed that it would come within the lifetime of their generation. 'We shall not all sleep,' writes St. Paul, and writes in haste with trembling hands because the time is short, 'we shall not all sleep, but we shall all be changed, in a moment, in the twinkling of an eye, at the last trump: for the trumpet shall sound, and the dead shall be raised in corruptible, and we (who are alive) shall be changed.' 'For this we say unto you by the word of the Lord, that we who are alive, that are left unto the coming of the Lord, shall in no wise precede them that are fallen asleep. For the Lord Himself shall descend from Heaven with a shout, with the voice of the archangel, and with the trump of God: and the dead in Christ shall rise first: and then we that are alive, that are left, shall together with them be caught up into the clouds, to meet the Lord in the air: and so shall we ever be with the Lord.'

To him that picture was a reality, a certainty, perhaps the greatest of all certainties, to him and to the Christians of his day, and so they lived - lived as men for whom the time was short; earth was not their home, its sunlit lanes and flowery fields held for them no sure abiding-place. They were as men who haste to gather in the harvest, with many an anxious look towards the sky, before the storm-cloud bursts and the thunders of God's judgment roll out across the world. They lived, urging men in season and out of season to escape the awful fate awaiting them if they were unprepared for that great day - the day of the Wrath of the Lord. Ever in their ears were the sounds of His coming - the beating of His Feet was in the air; every morning there was the chance that before the evening shadows fell the great last post, which was to be for the elect the great Reveille, would sound across the world and summon its millions to the valley of decision.

Life was to them indeed the great adventure - a tremendous and thrilling romance. Time pressed, the choice was urgent and compelling. Good and evil were not merely matters of life and death, they held an issue of more awful moment still. Men must choose, and choose now, or - words could not say, nor pictures represent, the horrors of that dread alternative.

It was as though those awful days of 1914, when, like a cruel and relentless sea, the German host was sweeping across Belgium on to Paris,

117

were the normal and not the abnormal atmosphere of life. There was a continual sense of a present crisis, the air was electric with expectation, and the Christian teachers cried with passionate and peremptory insistence, 'Now is the accepted time, now is the day of Salvation.'

Time passed on, and days stretched into months and years, and still the Heavens showed no sign. Suns rose and set, and stars shone steady in the sky; seed-time and harvest did not fail; the great world's life went rolling on. Feasting and fasting, loving and hating, sinning and repenting, laughing and weeping bitter tears - there was no change. Men began to mock the urgency of the Christian hope, and their yet more urgent dread. 'Where is the promise of His coming?' they cried, 'for from the days when the Fathers fell asleep all things continue as they were from the beginning of Creation.' But the Christian teachers replied, 'Forget not this one thing, Beloved, that one day with the Lord is as a thousand years, and a thousand years as one day.' The Lord is not slack concerning His promise as men count slackness, He is long suffering, not willing that any should perish, but that all should come to repentance.

Men grew impatient then. I wonder what they would have felt could they have seen into the future, could they have seen full twenty centuries roll out before them, and watched the little handful of men and women that was their world double itself and double itself again and again until the great earth groaned with its modern multi-millions. If the veil could have been lifted from their eyes, and they, standing upon some pinnacle of eternity, could have seen the fields of time stretch out before them - fields stained with blood, torn with war, foul with the filth of sin, and made hideous by corruption, and yet shot through with gleams of glory, and with the splendour of unselfishness and heroic sacrifice - would even the Christians have still felt as they did, would it still have been sufficient for them to reply that with God a thousand years were as one day, and one day as a thousand years? Would they have been able to maintain in themselves and in their followers that sense of expectation and of urgency, that feeling that they lived in a time of perpetual crisis which called upon them and the nations of the world for an immediate and conclusive choice?

This much is certain, that we have not been able to maintain it, at any rate on those grounds. With the vast majority of Christian people it has been lost altogether; you will not find one man in a thousand who believes in any real sense that the end of the world might come tomorrow. Christian preachers have from time to time wrestled to revive that sense of urgency, and to convince people that all life is a crisis, and that they must choose, and choose without delay, or face some dread alternative. But as a rule, their efforts to revive the sense of crisis have taken a somewhat different form; instead of appealing to the Second Coming and the judgment as a certainty, instead of crying out to men that the sounds of His coming were in the air, and that they could hear already the beating of the angels' wings, they have appealed to the more definite and human certainty, that in the midst of life we are in death, that at any moment death might come to any one of us and summon him to meet his God.

The urgency of death took the place of the Second Coming, and by its terrors preachers have striven to force upon men the fact that they stood at the parting of the ways, and that if they failed to choose, and choose aright, now, they must make up their minds that when death knocked at the door it would lead them out to the certainty of ghastly and eternal torture. Preachers gave rein to their imaginations in their desire to make this terror felt; they depicted with every detail of awful imagery the scene of the Great Assize, and the relentless voice of the Great judge pronouncing His just sentence of eternal punishment. The Protestant preachers, in their reaction against the abuse of it, neglected almost entirely the merciful and reasonable doctrine of an Intermediate State or Purgatory, and in their earnest desire to make men feel that they must choose now, taught men to believe that the soul must pass straight from the dying body into the presence of God. But even for the Catholics the mercies of Purgatory were only for those who had made some choice, some definite surrender and confession of belief, before the moment of death. Both Protestants and Catholics attached tremendous importance to the making of one's peace before the end. Men and women whose minds were reeling and shaken with disease or distraught with pain were feverishly urged by priests to repent them of their former sins, and to trust in Jesus Christ, and were taught that if they failed to make surrender in time, they must face the certainty of bitter and absolutely endless torment.

There still lingers among many people a horror of allowing their loved ones to pass out into the Great Unknown without some definite confession of faith. It still lingers, but only lingers, and appears to be dying away. Ought we to revive it? Ought we to urge upon people the tremendous and paramount importance of making their peace with God before they die, and the certainty of awful consequences if they fail to do it?

There has been in these last days a wide-spread and almost universal revolt among Christian men and women against the doctrine of eternal punishment. Thousands of good Christian people feel that it is impossible to reconcile with the Love of God those visions of endless torment with which the teaching of the past is filled. The fear of Hell has lost its hold upon our people, and lost its reality for our preachers. They no longer appeal to it, and if they did, it is fairly certain that only a small number would respond.

One sermon upon Hell-fire I have heard preached within the last five years - a sermon terrible in its earnestness, preached to men just about to go up the line - and what struck me as horrible about the result of it was that the men who came up to the penitent-form afterwards were mostly nervous and unhealthy-looking boys, who looked like neurasthenics, and who, manifestly carried away by the atmosphere, were clammy and sweating with fear, and I am afraid not half so much fear of the eternal as fear of battle and all it meant. Even in those dreadful times I could not bring myself to do it. I could not have preached that sermon, because I simply could not believe in that awful dilemma which lay at its root; and if I could have preached it, I believe the result would have been the same, to frighten a lot of weakly and neurotic people, and leave the bronze-faced, healthy, gallant crowd of men whose souls I desired to save untouched and somewhat disgusted. I have watched many of these men die in hospital and on the field, and I cannot remember a single case in which a man was afraid of the Hereafter. Wounds they feared, and pain, and always they were loath to loose their hold on life, but never have I met a man who feared the Great White Throne and the voice of the relentless Judge.

Am I to take this as part of the Church's failure to convince men of the great realities, as part of the widespread heathenism among the men of to-day which is the reproach of the Gospel? Ought I to go down upon my knees and repent, not merely of their failure to grasp that awful alternative, but of my own failure to grasp it, and to realise the hold it ought to have on my own life? For that, of course, is where the failure lies. One cannot preach as reality to others what is not reality to oneself, and the fear of pain and torture Hereafter is not reality to me, and does not play any part in my daily life. I do not turn from evil because it may land me in Hell - the Hell of endless pain - and I am not, and never have been, afraid of death, though I am as afraid of pain and wounds and blood as most men.

Of course, what I feel and believe is absolutely of no importance except so far as I am an ordinary typical man of my own time, but that is just what I believe I am, and so if this fact, that men are not afraid of the Hereafter and of endless torture, is a sign of heathenism, then, Dear Lord, I am a heathen too, because I do not fear it. And yet I am perfectly certain that if you try to tear out of the New Testament, and out of the teaching of the Christ, the element of solemn warning and the sense of life as a time of real crisis, a time when a choice must be made, fraught with appalling consequences; if you try to take the judgment out of the teaching of Christ, then you must invent a new Christ and a new New Testament. This sense of Crisis in Life is an essential part of the Christian consciousness. It is here that the belief in movement and progress as the essence of God's universe comes to my help. I cannot believe that there is any limit to God's Love, or that ever, either in this world or in the next, could He cease to seek and to save that which is lost. I cannot believe that it could ever be His Will that a single soul should remain in eternal torment, but I do perceive that men are, to a certain extent, free, and that they can wilfully reject God's Love and spurn it, and I do perceive that there is a *possibility* that they may go on wilfully rejecting it, not only in this life, but in the life to come. I perceive, too, that every time you reject it, it becomes harder to accept it - harder even to see it and realise it at all. I do perceive that men are not so much 'beings' as 'becomings,' that life is motion up or down, up towards good or down towards evil, and that every choice is a step one way or other.

And it is along these lines that the sense of the urgency of life comes back to me. It is in the light of modern knowledge that the meaning of those awful record books becomes quite plain and clear. Psychological research has revealed the fact that every impression, however slight, is recorded with infallible accuracy in the depths of the sub-conscious mind. Every thought, every word, every deed makes its impression there, an impression which is recorded with an accuracy almost beyond belief. And so in the motion of the mind, which is its life, every thought, word, and deed plays its part *in deciding the direction of the movement,* whether it be towards life or death. This fact it is which restores to me the sense of perpetual crisis. It is not so much for me that I may waken to-morrow to find the Great White Throne set up in the mists of the morning, and hear the sound of the angels' trumpets and the call to the judgment Seat, it is not so much that the judgment may come to-morrow *as that it is coming to-day.* The Day of judgment is to me not so much an act in time as a process in eternity. That tremendous picture of the Great Assize, of the Judgment Throne, with all the nations of the world gathered before it, is to me not so much a picture of to-morrow as a picture of to-day *and to-morrow and the Beyond.*

When Christ, in a lightning flash of vision, saw Himself coming on the clouds of glory to judge the world, He summed up the history of the ages and expressed it in one act, just as He did when the seventy returned with their tales of evil subdued, and in the light of that feeble beginning He discerned infinite possibilities, and said that He saw 'Satan as lightning fall from Heaven,' thus summing up in one tremendous picture the agelong battle of the Church Militant here on earth against sin, disease, and war.

That is precisely what I believe these visions of the judgment Day really mean; they are the summing up in vivid and compelling pictures of the essential meaning of the history of the world. This is the profoundest truth that lies behind the doctrine of the Day of judgment; every day is judgment Day, and Jesus Christ is always judge, because He is Perfect Man - the Son of Man. He is what we are made to be, and so must be our Judge. It is not that another Christ, different in form, clothed with a different glory, will come some day, it is that the same Christ, clothed with the same glory - the glory of His dreadful humility, of His love, and of His sacrifice - is coming to-day and every day to judge the world, is coming to judge the quick and the dead, the souls in this life and in the life beyond.

Every day you and I write our records out upon the tablets of our mind; every day the Perfect Man stands in very deed to judge them, good or bad, not by any arbitrary act, but because He is the Perfect Man towards Whom the mind must move if it is to find life, and from Whom, as it moves, it must draw nearer death. He is the judge of the movement of our lives, as the harbour mouth is the judge of the direction of a ship that sails, and every sin is a swerving from the point a swerving which must be retraced, or life can never find its haven and its rest. If the soul continues to move away from Him, away from Life, if we wilfully keep it on a wrong course, it can only steer to its destruction. What the destruction of the soul actually means, it is impossible to say, but I feel very intensely that it is a possible and appalling fate fraught with awful consequences, and so I feel as one who holds the rudder of a ship tearing through the water at a blinding pace, with the storm-winds of passion in its sails, knowing that every turn, however slight, of the rudder may mean either disaster or the intensely difficult task of retracing the distance lost.

There stands the inevitable Jesus, the inevitable Goodness to which I must come if I am to find life. To Him my life must move or be dashed upon the rocks, and every choice is of intense importance, every thought or word or deed of evil is a turning from the course to which the whole being responds as quickly and inevitably as a perfect yacht responds to its rudder, and the result of which is registered with the same awful, but perfectly natural, accuracy as a turning is marked for the ship upon the sea. So it is that without any exaggeration the sense of crisis is restored, restored to me from the pages of scientific text-books on the study of the mind.

And in the light of this knowledge, the world, as it lives to-day, appears to me in my moments of vision to be as mad, as recklessly and criminally mad, as it must have seemed to the early Christians. The way men will fly at once to a doctor when the slightest sign of disorder appears in their bodies, but will allow their minds to go tearing through life, tossed and torn by every passing passion, swept out of their course by every crazy doctrine, and will never make an attempt to change their direction or set them right by any noble standard, seems like the recklessness of lunatics. The strenuous efforts we make to stamp out diseases of the body, the money we spend, and the trouble we will take to stay the course of a physical epidemic, while we allow diseased and morbid teaching to be spread broadcast among our people, debauching and degrading their minds by continual suggestions of evil, which are allowed to play upon their imaginations without check - all this, to one who knows the power of suggestion and the inevitable laws of its working, seems like the carelessness of criminals. Only a mad world would spend thousands on curing venereal disease, and allow scoundrels to make thousands out of breeding it by ingenious suggestion.

I feel come upon me all the urgency of the old prophet crying to men that they are fools - mad fools and blind - sailing gaily to their destruction. It is not any eternal torment of the body that I fear for them and for myself, it is not any punishment for sin that I dread; *it is sin itself, the disease.* It is the festering sores of lust and pride and selfishness, the foul mattering of sin upon the soul, that I hate. It is simply the corruption of the mind which results from sin that to me is Hell.

I do not think there can be any judgment sense for a man, any realisation of the awful crisis, until he has seen Christ. *You cannot make a man fear Hell really until you have made him love God.* Once again you must take the challenge in its order, and the judgment comes at its end, and not at its beginning. You cannot drive men to the vision of God by the fear of Hell, but you can reveal to men the meaning of Hell by the love of God. It is the vision of the Jesus order of goodness, and its inevitability, that makes men see the horror of the gates of Hell; and it is the knowledge that every thought, word, and deed is a step either upwards towards that shining vision or downwards towards that damnable abyss of sordid, mean futility, it is that that makes every day a judgment day indeed.

But there is more than that, because as I look upon the story of my own mind and the story of the mind of the world, I see that the movement of both is like the movement of a great river, flowing on for the most part in the dark, but which now and then comes to a time of storm, when vivid flashes of lightning reveal which way it flows.

For long periods the mind of the ordinary careless man and the mind of the ordinary careless woman moves on its course without any revelation of where it is going to, and then there comes a crisis, a day of special judgment.

A man lives a life of quite ordinary immorality, not any more nor not any less animal than that of the set in which he moves; he lives as his companions live; and then one day he gathers up into his arms a little baby born blind, and knows that he struck out its eyes, and he stands revealed to himself for what he is - a dirty, foul-minded blackguard. Out of the sightless eyes of his own child Christ stares and cries, 'Inasmuch as ye have done it unto the least of these My little ones, ye have done it unto Me.' It is his judgment day. Every thought and every word and every deed of his past life has played its part in bringing him there to stand before the baby's throne and hear his sentence read, and Jesus, the Man Divine, is the Judge.

And so to different men in different ways, sometimes in the form of a great responsibility which they cannot bear, sometimes in the form of a great opportunity which they cannot take, sometimes in the form of a crowning temptation which they cannot resist, comes the day of crisis - they are called to their judgment. And as it is with individual men and women, so it is with nations. For years their history rolls on in the dark, and they cannot, and will not, see whither it is going, because they reject the only Light by which they can see, reject Him Who is the Light of the world; and then there comes a day of crisis, and they are made to see. Just such a Day of judgment has this Western world been through in these last years. For a century the life of Europe rolled on, with its vulgar commercialism, its sordid money-grabbing, its cruelty to children, its exploitation of the weak, its tyrannies and oppressions, blinded by its surface prosperity and its idiotic trust in force, building its battle-ships and torturing its women, bloated with pride and self-sufficiency, counting its wealth, and pointing at its wonderful enterprise, its growth in knowledge, and its supreme command of the forces of nature; and then came the Day of Judgment. In the flashlight of a million guns, in the groans of dying men and the wailing of countless widows, in the agony and bloody sweat of a continent racked with pain, we were made to see whither we had been going, and what it meant. Christ came to judge. Not that He willed it, not that He sent it, but that *we* willed it, and *we* made it, and He came to judge, not changed in form, not clothed in any other raiment, but just Jesus, the same yesterday, to-day, and for ever. He, Humanity Incarnate, stood in the midst of its battle-fields and judged.

I am not indulging in fancy, but am merely true to fact, when I say that I have seen Him standing there time and time again, pointing His loving but relentless Finger to the dead man at my feet, and saying, 'That is what it means. That is what "business is business," that is what "free and unfettered competition," that is what refined materialism and Godless prosperity really mean - that boy with the swollen, shapeless face, with the great hole in his head and the brain tumbling out, that is what they really mean. This is the Day of Judgment.' That is the vision that we ought to have seen, but have we? Has one in a million seen it? Would one in a million believe it if they could see it now? And yet it is true, as true as Truth. My God, cannot we see that it is mad to let our lives and the lives of our people go tearing across the sea of history without a light to guide them, without a standard by which to judge the course they steer? Can we not see that Godless diplomacy, Godless commerce, and Godless pleasure are worse than crimes; they are stupid, sinful blunders. We must have light. There is no other light, there is no other standard, than that which shines in His Face. We must see it, and we must guide our ships towards it, or we must perish on the rocks; and as I write the rocks are near, and I can hear the breakers beating on a cruel shore, and I cry with the sense of crisis on me, as the first Christians cried, 'Now is the accepted time, and now is the day of Salvation.' Mr. Thomas spoke more truly than he knew when he said, 'We shall either be on the rocks or off them in six months.'

But there is more still, because as each day of judgment reveals the meaning of all other days that have preceded it, and sums up in a flash the history of a man or the history of a continent, so it seems to me that some day there must come a great judgment Day, a great crisis, which will sum up the meaning of all history, from its strange beginning to its far-off and inconceivable end - a great day when the meaning of every evil thing shall be finally revealed, and in that flash of revelation perish and come to an end. And in that day, if there is a soul or a community of souls that have wilfully rejected the love of the Father, and wilfully refused to see the Light, then it seems inevitable that they must perish and lose for ever the chance of attaining life. From that day a new and wonderful movement must begin, the movement of pure goodness, untainted by evil, towards the beatific Vision and the splendour of His Face. And so, because of the facts of history, and because of the faithfulness of God, and the working of His eternal laws which govern the mind, I believe very intensely that 'He shall come again at the end of the world to judge both the quick and the dead.'

I cannot, and I dare not, picture that Great Assize; I cannot, and I dare not, try to realise the form that it will take; but I feel in my bones that it must come, and that every thought, word, and deed of every man that lives or ever has lived makes certain of its coming. I have my vision of judgment, and it has its own fear; it is not the fear of a flaming Hell, it is the fear of the Eyes of Christ, and by the splendour of those Eyes I plead with myself and with you that we live our lives in the fear and the love of God.

'I saw no thronged angelic court, I saw no great white throne,
I saw no open judgment books, I seemed to stand alone.
I seemed to stand alone beside a solemn sounding sea,
While at my feet upon the shore broke waves of memory.
Their murmuring music sobbed and sought a way into my soul,
The perfect past was present there, and I could see it whole,
Its beauty and its ugliness, its sorrow and its sin,
Its splendour and its sordidness, as wave on wave rolled in.
And ever deeper pierced the pain of all that I had lost,
My dear dead dreams of perfect things, I saw them tempest-tossed.
They fell like wreckage at my feet, and, as I turned them o'er,
The solemn waves, in Memory's caves, kept booming "Nevermore!"
There came one dream, more dear than all, a corpse without a head,
The flying spray hissed "Cowardice," and it was dead. cold dead.
Then suddenly a shadow fell, and I was not alone,
He stood with me beside the sea, and listened to its moan.
I did not dare to raise my eyes, I feared what I might see,
A cold sweat broke and bathed my brow, I longed to turn and flee,
But could not; rooted there I stood, in shiv'ring shame and fear;
The subtle shadow substance took, and nearer came, and near.
O was it days or was it years we stood beside that sea,
Or was it æons, timeless times? It seemed eternity.

At last, compelled, I raised my eyes. Two eyes looked into mine,
And shattered all my soul with shame, so sad and so divine.
It palsied all my pride with pain, the terror of those tears,
And wrought into my soul the woe of all my wasted years.
"Depart from me," I cried, "Depart, I cannot stand with Thee
And face the sorrow of those eyes beside this cruel sea.
Depart from me, I dare not tread the sands those feet have trod,
Nor look into those eyes that tell the agony of God.
For there is written all the tale of my soul's trait'rous tryst,
The sordidness of sin that seared the splendid eyes of Christ."
"Depart," I cried, and He was gone. I stood there all alone,
In silence save that Memory's sea still made perpetual moan.
Night shadowed all, and wandering winds came wailing from afar,
But out across the darkening sea shone forth one single star.'

I fear the day that may come for me and for my people, when there would not even be the star.

Printed in the United Kingdom
by Lightning Source UK Ltd.
134135UK00003BA/5/A